Critical Thinking Secrets

Discover the Practical Fundamental Skills and Tools That Are Essential to Improve Your Critical Thinking, Problem Solving, and Decision Making Skills

Table of Contents

Chapter 1: Introduction 3

Chapter 2: What is Critical Thinking and Why is it Important? 6

Chapter 3: Skills You Will Develop 21

Chapter 4: Why Critical Thinking? 32

Chapter 5: Practical Ways to Improve Critical Thinking 48

Chapter 6: How to Implement Critical Thinking 83

Chapter 7: Common Critical Thinking Pitfalls and How to Avoid Them 139

Chapter 8: How Critical Thinking Affects Your Life 225

Chapter 9: Conclusion 230

Chapter 1: Introduction

Critical thinking is the ability to analyze facts and information to make rational decisions, and understand the logical connection between ideas. It also involves the ability to engage in reflective and independent thinking. Critical thinking is a complex subject and there are a lot of definitions given to it. In general, it is the ability to evaluate factual evidence to make decisions rationally by making use of the information available.

Critical thinking is more about using available information based on experience and facts to solve problems and knowing where to find it. A person who has a good memory and knows many things does not imply that he or she can think critically. Gathering information is one thing, using it effectively is another.

Though its name seems to suggest otherwise, critical thinking does not imply being argumentative or critical of others. It can be used in avoiding fallacies, bad reasoning, and it can also play a very significant role in cooperative reasoning and constructive tasks. It can make our arguments more compelling, in addition to helping us gather facts and knowledge. Moreover, critical thinking can also be used to improve our work processes and enhance social institutions.

Those with good critical thinking skills can:
- Reflect on the justification of one's own beliefs and values
- Recognize the relevance and necessity of ideas
- Fix problems systematically
- Identify inconsistencies and common reasoning mistakes
- Recognize, create, and assess arguments

- Understand the logical connections between ideas

Of course, we are not gifted with the ability to make good decisions and reach appropriate conclusions all the time.

The primary tool that we use in making better judgments is critical thinking. Basically, critical thinking is the careful application of reasoning in determining whether or not a claim is true.

Developing the willingness and the ability to apply the critical thinking skills found in this book will make you smarter and help you improve your critical thinking skills with actual practical advice and strategies. The things and lessons that you are going to learn from this book can be applicable to the everyday decisions that you make in your life.

Chapter 2: What is Critical Thinking and Why is it Important?

There are many different definitions for critical thinking, and generally, all of them emphasize the importance of clarity and rationality in the way we think. Critical thinking is the process of using reasoning to find out what is true and what is false. It plays a very important role in our daily lives because we all make decisions every day, both small and big. After getting up from bed in the morning, we all have to make the decision on what to eat for breakfast, what to wear for the day and more. These are very simple and common decisions that we constantly make. Moreover, we also make decisions that can really have an impact on our lives. These life-changing decisions include, for example, selecting a university in which to pursue higher education or choosing the person to love and marry, etc.

Critical thinkers approach any circumstance in a way that ensures every possible solution is within their control or is something they know of. To put it simply, critical thinking is the process of applying what you know to reach the best possible solution.

Critical thinking is a way of thinking about particular things at a particular time, and it is not about gathering facts and knowledge or something that you can learn once and use it forever.

When we think critically, we can analyze information without bias or prejudice and make decisions accordingly. It also involves the assessment and evaluation of sources such as data, facts, and other phenomena. When we can think critically, we will be able to draw reasonable conclusions from the data, facts, or information and evaluate the information to arrive at the best possible solution to fix a problem or make a decision.

The idea of critical thinking has been the centerpiece of most research in the last 50 years. The words themselves are derived from Greek. "Critical" comes from "kriticos," which means discerning judgment and "kriterion," which means standards. Therefore, the word implies the development of "discerning judgment based on standards."

It is our nature for everyone to think. However, much of our thinking tends to be biased, partial, distorted, and uninformed. The quality of life that we produce depends on the quality of our thoughts. If we think correctly and critically, we can improve the quality of our lives. Badly-constructed thoughts are costly both in money and in quality of life. Better thoughts must be cultivated.

Critical thinking is a mode of thinking about a problem, content, or subject where the thinker wants to improve their thinking skill by skillfully analyzing, evaluating, and reconstructing it.

People who possess well-cultivated critical thinking skills are able to:

- Raise important questions and problems
- Formulate the questions and problems clearly and precisely
- Accumulate and evaluate information using an effective interpretation of abstract ideas that lead to well-reasoned conclusions and feasible solutions
- Think freely with the alternative system of thought
- Communicate effectively with others in finding the solutions to complicated problems

Summary of TheConceptualization of Critical Thinking

Critical thinking is self-guided thinking that attempts to give a reason at the highest level of quality in an equitable way. People who want to make decisions rationally and reasonably have to think critically and consistently. They are always reminded of the mistakes that human beings make if they do not check carefully before making decisions. They try to decrease the power of their egocentric and socio centric inclinations and use their own knowledge and what critical thinking offers such as concept and principles to help them improve their thinking skills. These people also know that there are always new things they can learn, no matter how good they are as critical thinkers. There are always other fallacies and mistakes they can make, and irrationalities, prejudices, biases, etc., that they can discover and challenge. They try to improve the world however they can to contribute to a more rational human society.

10 Traits of Critical Thinkers

What is a good critical thinker? What are the characteristics of ideal critical thinkers?

1. Spirit of Inquiry
   Effective critical thinkers are broadly interested and generally curious to know more about a wide range of topics. They are more likely to be curious about the world and people. Being able to understand and appreciate the differences in culture, beliefs, and opinions is another good characteristic of great critical thinkers.

2. Empathy
   There is already enough judgment and separation in the world. As we all want to help other people to acquire critical

thinking skills, we should not ignore that critical thinking also needs to be emotional and instinctual as much as it is intellectual. That is why critical thinkers need to act with their hearts along with their minds.

3. Be Aware

   We need to be aware that we can stop and think about something critically at any moment. Good critical thinkers are always ready and alert for an opportunity to use their best critical thinking skills in any situation. This enthusiasm to think critically about even the simplest problems and tasks shows the desire for constructive results.

   Critical thinking also means that we do not accept something easily, but we look and explore all sides of the issue and remain curious to know more about the facts.

4. Be Decisive

Many situations require you to be quick and decisive, especially those that involve critical thinking. When we apply critical thinking in solving problems, we will weigh our options and expect results at the moment with speed and clarity. Effective critical thinkers are also able to put away their fear when making decisions because they are sure about the decisions they are going making and the results that they are going to get. Critical thinkers do not like to keep things backward, and they always try to move forward and avoid procrastination. Moreover, we have to make decisions even though we still do not have enough information that is needed to make decisions with confidence. When we are faced with such a problem, we become uncertain and let those who are making the final decision make it, although they may not know as much as you do. Effective critical thinkers always understand, more or less, that they will have to make decisions even though they realize that they may end up making the wrong ones. If possible, they would rather not decide at all.

5. Be Honest

Honesty is important, especially in critical thinking. Effective critical thinking includes things such as moral integrity, ethical consideration, and actions. However, honesty remains at the core of all these things. People with honesty have a strong desire for harmony in the world and to attain this outcome requires honesty in all relationships and collaborations between human beings.

How we look within ourselves to accept what is there is also the practice of honesty in critical thinking. Critical thinkers also equally see themselves as other people.

6. Have Willingness

   In the following things, we will need the willingness to:
   - We have to learn from our own personal mistakes and faults
   - We have to challenge the situation where needed
   - We have to be open-minded and accept the opinions of other people
   - We also have to think about their opinions and views with the introduction of new evidence
   - We have to be active listeners

   We have to always keep improving, learning, and performing well

7. Be Creative

   It is true that effective critical thinkers are often creative thinkers. Creativity is really essential in business, marketing, and other professional careers. These kinds of jobs rely heavily on creativity. When businesses are able to produce creative products and effective advertisement, their business will be able to run into the global marketplace.

8. Persistence

   Staying focused on the task with great perseverance is something that effective critical thinkers need to do, and they know that it is essential to do so. It is the nature of critical thinkers not to give up easily until the solution to the problem is found and the decision is reached. Here, we can say critical thinkers tend to possess a leadership mindset in the way they think about solving problems. This quality trait is not only useful to have but also encourages others in a team-working environment.

9. Be Objective

   Another trait of critical thinkers is to focus on fairness and inclusion of all sides of opinion and concerns. There is no bias in critical thinking, but only embracing and consideration of possibilities. People with critical thinking skills will not allow themselves to be affected by external influences and internal ones like their emotions or feelings.

10. Reflective Ability

    When we are talking about critical thinking, our focus will not simply stop after making decisions and having the outcome. It will be an important area for improvement and reflection on the learning journey for critical thinkers. We should never ignore our own personal mistakes, but should not live with them. We have to learn from them and move on to the next challenge.

Critical thinking is active, purposeful, mindful, logical, and persistent as opposed to passive, superficial, negligent, illogical, and irresolute.

Benefits of Critical Thinking

With the help of this book, you too can become a more rational thinker. Benefits of critical thinking include:

- Approach: One of the most important learning developments in critical thinking is awareness. This includes being aware of the different approaches to a problem and objectively assessing whether they are viable. Relying on a standard, uniform problem-solving method sets the baseline for problem-solving so that you can get creative and find other, better approaches to increase your chance of success.
- Save time: With a critical thinking mindset, you can tell from the start which information is irrelevant to

whatever you are trying to accomplish. Many people tend to be overwhelmed with too much information from the get-go, so knowing what is relevant to your task saves you a lot of time. Plus, you know that you make a good decision because you use only the data that matters.

- Appreciation for different views: Critical thinking requires you to think objectively on all the views regarding a scenario. You will develop an appreciation of different views because you learn how to judge cultural norms and understand other factors that can influence decision-making. This is a fundamental element in effective teamwork and leadership.
- Better communication: Because critical thinking requires you to analyze and build up facts to support your claim in any given premise, you can become a more effective communicator. You

become more aware of communication cues and are able to adapt to them properly. Moreover, when you know your facts and how they line up, you can proceed to present them in a consistent manner, which is pivotal when you are presenting a proposal or idea.

- Decision making: This is rather obvious, but critical thinking leverages your decision-making abilities to another level. You leave intuition or guesswork behind and go into a more analytical and in-depth basis, which leads to better decisions.

- Reason: Being able to reason is also crucial because all your presentations and ideas will be challenged, so you need to defend them. Here, you will learn how to make inductive and deductive reasoning as well as when to use them. Your decisions will be built on reason and logic rather than on emotion or instinct.

Chapter 3: Skills You Will Develop

In this chapter, we take a look at some of the most essential critical thinking skills you should and will develop after going through this book. We also discuss some of the things you can do to improve each skill, although you will find a more in-depth guide in a later chapter.

Crucial Critical Thinking Skills

Many skills fall under the critical thinking umbrella, but we have grouped them into six for your convenience. Focusing on these can help you on your journey to becoming a better critical thinker.

Identification

You need to identify what you are dealing with first before you proceed to approach the problem. This means identifying the root cause or the factors that may influence the situation as well as the situation itself. After getting a lay of the land, you can then proceed to figure out how to improve the situation.

When presented with a problem or scenario, stop and access the situation thoroughly by asking the following questions:

- Who is doing what?
- What is the reason for this happening?
- What are the results? How can they be changed?

Research

There is this common knowledge that you should drink eight bottles of water a day or some similar figures. It does not take a veteran critical thinker long to figure out that this fact is ambiguous at best because it does not specify the exact volume of water you should be drinking. Do you know where this figure comes from? Researchers who came up with this result were actually funded by companies that sell water bottles. See the problem?

So, when you need to compare arguments about something, make sure that the research behind those arguments is independent because arguments are intended to be persuasive and certain facts and figures presented in their favor may actually lack context or come from unreliable sources. The best way to approach this problem is verification by finding the source of the information and evaluating whether they are presented objectively. So, how do you improve this field?

First, develop a habit of spotting unsourced claims. Does the person making that argument cite where they got their facts and figures from? If you ask them or try to find it yourself, but got no clear answer, then this is already a red flag. Moreover, it is worth noting that not all sources are equally valid. There is a difference between popular and scholarly articles, for example. This is basically the difference between science and "pop science."

Popular articles are intended for the general public and are generally shorter. This means that certain information is glossed over and some are so simplified that some technical details are missing. Again, this is for the general public so the language is simple and easy for general readers to understand and the article may contain photographs, graphics, or visuals to help readers understand. Such articles cover general interest topics or events, written by the publication's staff of journalists who may not have enough knowledge or experience in the field. While many articles are edited and information presented is fact checked, it may still be used incorrectly.

On the other hand, scholarly articles or academic journals are more comprehensive as they are written by scholars and researchers for academics, professionals, and experts in the field. The general public may not understand everything because these articles are longer and narrower in scope but provide in-depth analysis. These articles are even more complicated by the fact that technical or scholarly language is used, which may be too advanced for normal readers. The articles contain original research findings and other source materials are meticulously cited. Visuals-wise, you may find charts and graphs to help illustrate their findings. In addition to being edited and fact-checked, scholarly articles are peer-reviewed, meaning that panels of experts review submitted articles to ensure that the research process is valid and that the findings contribute something new to the field before finally publicizing them.

Identifying Biases

This is one of the hardest skills to master because even the best of us have some biases they are unaware of. Being good at critical thinking involves the ability to analyze information objectively. Think of yourself as a judge and you need to evaluate the validity of the claims of both sides of an argument while keeping in mind that biases may be present in there.

It is also important to learn how to set aside your own personal biases that might cloud your judgment, and that can be a very difficult task to accomplish. Another person may be able to identify a few biases that you have and this is why the decision-making body consists of more than one individual. In this context, you want someone to argue with so that you can reach a more objective decision. If no one is available, you can only argue with yourself. That is okay too because you can still challenge your own thoughts and assumptions. That way, it is still possible to see things from different viewpoints.

To improve this area, start by challenging yourself to identify evidence that forms your beliefs. Moreover, determine whether or not your sources are credible. Most importantly, remember that bias exists. When it comes to evaluating information or an argument, consider the following:

- Who will benefit from this?
- Does the source of this information appear to have an agenda?

- Is it overlooking, ignoring, or leaving out certain information that does not support its claims?
- Is the source using wordings in a way to sway an audience's perception of a fact?

Inference

Being able to infer and draw conclusions based on the information given is also key. The information you get does not always tell you explicitly what it means. Most of the time, you need to go through the raw data and then connect the dots on your own.

This skill allows you to extrapolate and identify potential results when assessing a scenario. Of course, because you need to use your own judgment to interpret data, the inference is not always correct. For instance, if you read that someone weighs 300 pounds, you may infer that they are overweight and unhealthy. However, when other data such as body composition and height are included, your conclusion may change.

So, how do you improve in this field? An inference is an educated guess because you try to make sense of the data you currently have. Here, your ability to infer correctly and accurately can be further enhanced by collecting as much information as possible before making conclusions. When you are faced with a new scenario or situation to evaluate, stop and try to skim for clues first. Look for things like headlines, images, features, and statistics and ask yourself what you think is going on.

Determining Relevance

One of the hardest parts of critical thinking is when you need to figure out what information is most important for you to consider. In most cases, you will have a plethora of information that may seem important to you, although it may turn out to be only a small fraction to consider.

To improve your ability to determine the importance and relevance of data, start by establishing a clear direction in what you are trying to figure out. What do you need to do? Do you need to find a solution? Should you be identifying a trend? If you know what your end goal is, you will have a clearer picture of what is actually relevant.

Even so, having an objective does not mean that the task is going to be much easier because you do not know for sure what is truly relevant. It's worth having a physical list of the things you look for based on the level of relevance. When you know what you want to look for and what to prioritize, you will have a list that has a few obviously relevant pointers and a few, not-so-relevant ones at the bottom. Then, you can narrow down your focus on the lower-ranked topics and reevaluate its importance.

Curiosity

It is convenient when you just sit back and take all the information presented to you at face value. But we all know how that is only going to lead to a disaster, especially when you need to make a decision at the end of the presentation. We are all born curious. Many parents can attest to the fact that children often ask them too many whys all the time. As we get older, we grow to keep that urge at bay and remain silent. While this can help us from being perceived as annoying, it prevents us from thinking critically.

Being curious is easy. Just make a conscious effort to ask open-ended questions about the things in your everyday life. From there, ask follow-up questions. This allows you to probe for more information.

Chapter 4: Why Critical Thinking?

The question is why do we have to learn critical thinking skills? Why do we need these skills? Why do we need to become good critical thinkers? Most people will say that the skills we need to be good critical thinkers are problem-solving, creativity, analytical thinking, communication, collaboration, and accountability. Still, every single one of these skills falls under a broad umbrella which is called the critical thinking capacity. Let's take a look:

- Critical thinkers can solve problems effectively as they can logically consider all options and arrive at the best possible solutions based on the information they have.
- Creative thinking goes hand in hand with critical thinking because they require the compilation of new

knowledge, simplification of ideas, and the identification of possibilities.
- Critical thinkers are analytical thinkers because they collect data and information from many sources and evaluate them from various angles. They are skilled at conceptualization, organization, and combination of knowledge.
- One of the important things of critical thinking is being able to embrace and value the opinions and views of other people. Moreover, critical thinkers always try to encourage others in constructive reflection that can help build bonds and inspire forward thinking in the team.
- Critical thinkers are excellent at communication as they are open-minded and more aware of others. Plus, their values and beliefs are shown by how well they communicate with others.

- Critical thinkers realize the usefulness of being selfless, ethical, and respectful of other cultures and belief systems. They work hard and try their best when interacting with other people.

Below is an excerpt from the World Economic Forum that describes the Future of Jobs released in 2016:

"The Fourth Industrial Revolution, which includes developments in previously disjointed fields such as artificial intelligence and machine learning, robotics, nanotechnology, 3D printing and genetics and biotechnology, will cause widespread disruption not only to business models but also to labor markets over the next five years, with enormous change predicted in the skill sets needed to thrive in the new landscape."

The world is changing rapidly and constantly. In the past, humanity was convinced that everything that could be invented had already been invented. When the computer was first made and become a household item, a 56K modem was deemed to be fast and 200MB of storage huge. However, nowadays, we even have 1TB in smartphone storage. It shows that the world is changing and developing day by day and we did not even realize at the time that something was invented. Nothing is constant in life. Our society is evolving rapidly by the day. Certain things will grow and change completely in the blink of an eye. That is why we need to have a strong, well-developed critical thinking ability that can serve us. In order to adopt these changes, we need to develop resilience as well as critical thinking skills.

We can go back to learn from the past, 50 or 30 years ago. In order to become successful, what did we think was necessary to live our lives and become successful? It is true that what we thought was necessary and needed in the past is no longer important to us now. The usefulness of certain things has changed based on time and how we are living. In addition, the way we communicate and share our ideas has also transformed. In the past, we did not have a smartphone and internet connection to send our messages across, but now, simply with the touch of a button, we can send the message and it takes a second. We also see each other's faces even when we are miles apart. The way we do our business and the consuming behavior of customers has also changed from generation to generation. Everything has its benefits and drawbacks. Changes brought about by technology and other events bring new problems and challenges that require you to think critically so you can cope with them.

Effective critical thinkers will think differently according to circumstances. However, after all, what we want to do is to make a decision as quickly as possible. It is just like when your car breaks down in rush hour traffic, or you are negotiating world peace. In such situations, you need to think critically. These two situations require critical thinking skills although they take place in vastly different settings with different things at stake. Still, they all require critical thinking ability and skills.

Critical Thinking at the Workplace

Every employer wants employees who can use their logical thoughts to evaluate a situation and come up with the best solution to solve a problem. People with good critical thinking skills at the workplace can be trusted to make decisions on their own.

In recent years, critical thinking abilities are becoming important in every industry and workplace. We can demonstrate our critical thinking abilities with keywords such as analytical, problem solving, creativity, etc., in our CV and cover letter and more importantly, during the interview.

Critical thinking can be used in the workplace, and it varies from industry to industry. For example:
- If you are working in the hospital as a doctor with a case in hand, you will have to analyze the case and start to evaluate whether the patient should be treated or not.

If you are a manager in a company, you will need to analyze customer feedback and information to develop your company by training your staff.

How to Demonstrate Skill

Firstly, you can write critical thinking keywords such as analytical, creativity, etc. in your CV. In the description of your work history, you can elaborate on the critical thinking abilities you have used in your previous workplace.

Secondly, you can also put critical thinking skills in your cover letter. You can mention one or two critical thinking skills and give some examples related to what you did previously in your last place of work.

Finally, you can show your critical skills keywords during the interview, which is the most essential step in getting a job. You can discuss with the interviewer and tell them you could solve a particular problem using critical thinking skills to fix it.

In some workplaces, they will give a test in regards to the use of critical thinking abilities. You will be given a case to solve. The interviewers are curious to know how you can use your critical thinking skills to find the best possible solution to solve the problems.

There are 5 must-have critical thinking skills:

- Analytical: Analytical skill is the ability to examine something carefully to see whether it is a problem. It helps people examine and interpret information as well as recognize the differences and similarities. People with good analytical skills often know which questions to ask to get more information from data analysis, information seeking reports, interpretations, and judgments.

- Communication: Communication is also very important because you will have to share your conclusion with your employers and colleagues once you find the best solution to the problem that the company is facing. You need to have good and effective communication skills to transfer the information and ideas found to inform your employers about what should be done in order to improve the situation. You will have to ask important questions, give assessments, seek collaborations, and explanations to express your opinions and ideas. You can successfully implement your findings by improving your interpersonal communication, giving presentations, and working in a team through verbal or written communication.

- Creativity: A certain level of creativity is often needed in critical thinking. With creativity, you might come up with good ideas and the best solution that no one has found before. Creativity may involve the creative eye. You will need to have cognitive flexibility, conceptualization, curiosity, imagination, abstract connection, and vision.

- Open-mindedness: In order to be able to think critically, you need to be able to place any assumption or judgment aside and only focus on analyzing the information you get. You have to be objective and assess the ideas without bias. Being open-minded means you have to embrace the different cultural perspectives, and be fair, humble, objective, and inclusive in your critical thinking.

- Problems-Solving: Problem-solving is vitally important in the critical thinking skills that involves analyzing a problem, generating, and implementing a solution. Then, you have to assess the success of the plan. Most employers do not just want employees who can only think about information critically, but they also need an employee who can actually come up with practical solutions.

Critical Thinking in College

Throughout your years in schools and college, critical thinking is hardly used even though one can never stress its importance enough. This is one of the reasons why so many students struggle when they get into the professional world. Many of them had a completely wrong attitude toward tackling a challenging problem, and life as a whole. Such attitudes include:

- Ignorant certainty. It is the belief that all questions have definite and correct answers. This is what most students believe. In many exams, questions have a clear answer, but that is not the case in real life. There is often a grey area between the white and black. Most meaningful questions do not have a straightforward answer. In some courses, we need to think critically about the material during our study.

Unfortunately, many students neglect this area.

- Naïve relativism: It is the belief that all arguments are equal and there is no truth. According to Roberts, this is a view that students tend to follow when they learn about the error of ignorant certainty. One part of critical thinking is to evaluate the validity of the argument, both your own argument and others'. Thus, we have to understand that in critical thinking, some arguments are better and some are awful.

In addition, critical thinking also allows students to form their own opinions and participate actively with the material more than just with the superficial level. In class, it is important to learn with your professors or classmates through meaningful discussion. If you just learn what is written in the book, you will never get far. Furthermore, critical thinking skills also allow you to come up with good, worthy arguments and use them to back up your ideas and opinions. If you plan to pursue higher education, original and critical thoughts are essential. As critical thinking involves evaluating information, it will also help you assess your own work. As a student, we all want better grades and good habits of mind. Without critical thinking, while you are in college, you will get somewhere, but you are not likely to be in a place where you desire.

Critical Thinking in The Real World

Critical thinking plays a very important role in the real world and it does not stop in college. The reason is:

- Critical thinking helps you develop intellectually throughout your life even after you graduate. Graduation does not mean that you should stop learning. If anything, it is only the first step in your learning process, as there is so much more to learn out there. The world is changing and you need to keep learning as much as you can to keep yourself relevant. When faced with new challenges and information, being able to think critically will help you evaluate and use it.

- Critical thinking will help you to make difficult decisions. In a decision-making process, it is hard to make an immediate decision when you have the ability to evaluate many available options. Critical thinking will allow you to compare the pros and cons of each option and you will have more options than you can think of.

- People will take advantage of you if you let others think for you, and judge everything at face value. You may be familiar with many advertisements whose promises seem too good to be true. The useless and harmful products they sell rely on the ignorance or false hope of buyers. When you have the ability to think critically, you can avoid getting caught and motivated to buy something from unethical companies and people.

- Critical thinking will also help increase your employment rate with better pay. A good employer will not only look for an employee who can find a solution to an existing problem but will also look for someone who can come up with the best solution to the problem that no one has thought of. To get a well-paying job, you will need critical thinking skills and ability after your graduation because it is a crucial ingredient to fixing problems and difficulties.

Chapter 5: Practical Ways to Improve Critical Thinking

In this chapter, we will go over some of the most practical ways you can improve your critical thinking skills.

Critical Thinking Exercise

The idea of real critical thinking exercise is to find the truth. It requires us to move away from traditional thinking in order to find the truth.

Critical thinking is like a muscle. It takes constant practice to improve it. Thinking critically and gathering knowledge and experience. How can we keep improving our critical thinking skills? How can we encourage people to continue improving their critical thinking skills for a lifetime?

Improving our critical thinking does not need hours of lesson planning or require special materials. Thinking critically yields many benefits but you just need to be curious and open-minded. Below are some strategies you can employ to help you improve your critical thinking skills in your everyday life.

There is no magical way to immediately improve our critical thinking, and it will take time to practice in a regular way.

Don't Waste Time

Have you ever noticed that when you waste time you get nothing out of it? It is true that everyone has had this experience in their lives, even those who are good critical thinkers. It is like nature where water waste and time waste is unavoidable. Many people have not used their time productively and sometimes, not even pleasurably. Thankfully, we can maximize productivity and minimize time wasted on trivial matters. For instance, you can take the time you would spend watching TV to plan your days ahead.

We have arranged some questions that you can use to review how you practice your thinking throughout the day:

- When did I make my worst thinking today? When did I make my best thinking?
- What kind of things did I spend time thinking about today?
- Did I figure out something from my thinking?
- Did I permit negative thoughts to frustrate me easily?
- If I had a chance to repeat my day, what would I want to do differently? Why?
- Did I do anything that benefits my long term goals?
- If I spent time thinking the same way as I did today for 10 years, would I have

achieved something important in my life at that time?

You need to spend more time going through all of them or just a few in order to carefully and internally think about your response and record it in your journal. The more you spend time practicing this, the better you will be and you will see more patterns emerging in your thinking habits.

Learn Something New Every Day

Continuing to learn for a lifetime is all about making the process of learning an ongoing journey. We just need to learn something new that we did not know before. You can start by asking yourself what you have been curious to know. Is there a question about something that you want to get an answer for? If so, go and chase it. Do not stop till you figure out the answer you are looking for. No matter how simple or unimportant the question might be to other people. Just do not take that into account. From this practice, you can accomplish two things at the same time. One is, you can fulfill your intellectual needs and second, you can develop your habit of curiosity.

No Boundaries for Learning

Never ever think that you are too old to learn something new or achieve something amazing. There are many famous people who have accomplished great things when they are old, so ignore your age and start learning something new. There is no age restriction for learning, particularly, in the process of improving critical thinking skills.

Always Question

Asking questions shows a sign of intelligence. Asking questions means you are curious to know more. In today's world, we should encourage our children to ask more questions to discover possibilities and opportunities. Questions are good and good questions are better. The core of critical thinking and lifelong learning is the ability to ask meaningful questions that can lead to constructive and useful answers. Encouraging people to learn with asking questions as the focus will ensure that we and our learners do not learn in one way. It is a highly interactive learning process when we exchange ideas and discuss through asking questions. As a result, we can develop a habit of curiosity by asking questions to look for other opinions and views, taking nothing for granted.

The following questions are used to improve critical thinking skills: Think of something that you have just been told by someone and after that ask yourself the questions below:
- Who?
- Do you know that person?

- Is that person in power?
- Is it important to know who told you this?

- What?
  - Is it a fact or an opinion?
  - Are all the facts provided?
  - Is there anything left out?

- Where?
  - Public or private?
  - Were you given a chance to respond?

- When?
  - Is there any reason for their opinion?
  - Are they trying to make someone look good or bad?

- How?
  - Happy, sad or angry?
  - Spoken or written?
  - Could you understand?

Active Listening

Active listening is really essential in critical thinking as you will have enough information from the speaker and by paying attention, you will come up with good questions that lead to getting more information. Some say that you have two ears and a mouth for a reason. A good listener lets others talk first before expressing his or her own ideas and opinions. According to a study from the University of Missouri, many people are weak listeners. It does not help when there are so many distractions, either. Most people think that listening is an easy thing to do, but it is actually very difficult, especially for active listening. In order to be an active listener, we need to have a conscious and concerted effort to hear words being said by the speakers and more importantly, we have to understand what is being said in their message. Moreover, it is also crucial to understand what the speaker wants or is striving to achieve in the conversation.

Improving Active Listening

Active listening skills like other communication skills can be learned, accomplished, and taught.

Talk less: This should be obvious because it is impossible to both talk and listen at the same time. Listen and do not try to talk or think of a reply just yet. Focus on what the speaker is saying to get a clear message. After that, you can respond. That way, you allow the speaker to say all that needs to be said so you can fully understand what they are trying to say.

Adopt a listening mode: Keep silent and pay attention to hear what they are saying.

Furthermore, keep the environment quiet and open your mind in a comfortable manner with engaging eye contact. At the same time, make sure you are responding appropriately. Active listening is meant to promote respect and understanding. When listening, you gain more information, data, perspective, and insights. Attacking the speaker now and putting them down does not help anyone. Of course, that does not mean you should just sit there and nod, either. This brings us to the next point.

Respond properly: Be candid, honest, and open in your response and assert your opinions respectfully. When you respond and provide your own opinions, keep in mind that yours can sound just as wrong to them as theirs to you. Remember what is important in the discussion: reaching an agreement on the best solution. So, it does not matter who is right. What matters here is that a good decision has been made that day. Plus, you are here to take in ideas and knowledge and the other person is there to share it. You can save the discussion until after the presentation. There will always be an opportunity to talk.

Make the Speaker Feel Comfortable: You have to show some gestures or signs of agreement in your listening. If you think that seating makes you both feel comfortable, you can arrange the seat for the conversation. Be aware of the environment in which you are communicating.

Avoid Distraction: This means you have to make sure that you keep your phone in silent mode, keep the TV screen or speaker off. If the speakers request privacy, you can hold the conversation in a private room and close the door.

Put Your Personal Prejudice Aside: It is difficult for most people, but we can tackle this issue through learning and practice. Interrupting people is considered rude and a waste of time because it only serves to infuriate the speaker and restricts a full understanding of the message. Therefore, allow the speaker to finish each point properly. In some cases, the speaker will pause, offering you the opportunity to ask a question. That is the time to speak. Also, never interrupt with a counter-argument.

Pay Attention to Their Tone: The tone of the speaker's words can sometimes enhance the meaning of the words and sometimes, it can hide the meaning of the words. Make sure, you know the difference.

Look for the Underlying Meaning: In our listening, we will hear words, of course, but it is not something we want to listen. What we want to listen to is the underlying meaning, not really the words. Therefore, at first, we have to listen for comprehension and second, for ideas.

Pay Attention to Non-verbal Language: People do not only communicate through verbal language, but they can also use body language and facial expressions. That is why it is important that we use eye contact in our conversation

Provide feedback: Sometimes, we may misunderstand what the speaker is trying to say because of our personal biases, assumptions, judgments, and beliefs. Listening actively means that you need to understand what is being said as intended by the speaker. To achieve this, simply paraphrase what is being said. Put what they said into your own words and confirm with the speaker whether you got their message right. If you do not quite get what the speaker is trying to say, ask clarifying questions. Moreover, summarize the speaker's comments now and again to confirm that the two of you are still on the same page.

Solve Just the Problem

As human beings, we have got so many problems at hand and little time to solve them. These problems can be at the workplace, at home, or in society. Problems that we create through our action and choice or happen independently without our influence do not go away on their own. The only thing that we can do is to solve them on one by one, one day at a time. Hopefully, we can avoid these problems in the future.

You can start solving a problem in one day, every day so that you can keep your focus on it with undivided focus.

You can consider the words of author and speaker Les Brown "If you've got a problem that either man or god can solve, then you ain't got no problem." So, there is no need to be worried about facing problems at all. They are inevitable and we can achieve more if we embrace and see them as the mundane things in life. We can move on to solve them with a positive attitude.

Now, let's take a look at one approach mapped out by authors Richard Paul and Linda Elder. In their approach, you will have the roadmap to solving a problem you want to face daily.

- You have to state the problem as clearly and precisely as you can.
- You have to understand your problem and know what you are dealing with, and you also need to put aside the other problems that you have no control over which saves you time to focus on the problem that you can actually solve.
- You need to figure out the information you need and actively discover it.
- You need to analyze and interpret the information you collect carefully.

- You need to also identify what you can do in the short term and long term. Figure out all the options for action and visualize the most appropriate solution you want to achieve.
- You have to evaluate your options, and take into account their pros and cons.
- You have to take up a strategic approach to the problem and follow through with it.
- You need to track your progress as you implement your actions and be ready to review and alter your strategy should the need arise. Plus, your strategy should be flexible enough to allow changes when more information is available to you.

Through all these five practices, it takes lots of time and practice to improve our critical thinking skills. In addition, you will see significant improvement of your critical thinking skills when you follow all of these simple activities and systems.

Improving Critical Thinking Every Day

Now you already know what critical thinking is and the steps and ways you can improve critical thinking, but what we want to talk about in this section is how we can keep practicing and improving our critical thinking skills. You will find practical and beneficial ways to keep improving your skills, and as you practice these ways every day, on and on, you will feel comfortable with critical thinking in your daily life.

As human beings, we are great and have the capacity to do almost anything. However, we tend not to make use of those capacities and live undeveloped. Improving critical thinking is like improving in any other aspect like in sports. Improvement is not likely to happen if there is no conscious commitment to learn and practice. If we take our thinking for granted, you will see nothing improve. It takes time for the development of critical thinking, and the result will not come overnight. It will develop gradually over time. How can we develop as critical thinkers? How can we keep improving and practicing over time in everyday life?

We have to understand that there are phases needed in developing our critical thinking skills

Phase1: The Unreflective Thinkers: they are not aware of the problems they are having in their thinking.

Phase2: The Challenged Thinkers; they know what problems they are having in their thinking.

Phase3: The Beginning Thinkers; they try to improve their thinking, but do not practice on a regular basis.

Phase4: The Practicing Thinkers; they begin to realize the necessity of regular practice.

Phase5: The Advanced Thinkers; they start to advance their thinking together with their regular practice.

Phase6: The Master Thinker: they are skilled at critical thinking that it becomes their habit to think critically.

How to Sharpen Your Logical Thinking Skills

We all know about Sherlock and his unparalleled logical thinking skills. Thankfully, this is something that we can all achieve with a little practice.

Of course, maybe a convoluted murder case is out of your league, but at least you can improve your logical thinking skills to a level that makes problem-solving and decision-making much easier. These skills will contribute to success in your personal and professional life. So, what can you do to sharpen your mind?

Learn the Terminology

Before you start brushing up on your logical thinking skills, it is worth knowing its set of terms and being acquainted with them. That way, the rest of the journey will be much easier. You need to know terms such as premise, assumption, conclusion, argument, observation, inference, various types of statement, etc.

Making Logical Conclusions

It does sound strange, but practice makes perfect. You do not need to get yourself into a difficult situation to improve your logical thinking skills. Trying to think in conditional statements and find causes and consequences of small and insignificant facts is enough. Basically, just identify the premise and conclusion in any conditional statement and establish a link between them.

For example, let us assume that if it is raining, it is cold outside. So, we have the statement: "If it is raining, it is cold outside." In a conditional sentence, if the premise is true, then the conclusion is also true. That's it. Just develop this kind of thinking with other things and see if the relationship works between the premise and conclusion.

Play Card Games

There are other ways to make the learning process fun. Why not gather your friends once every week to play a light-hearted card game to stimulate your brain to think quickly and logically? Challenging card games will only dampen the mood and make the learning process arduous. Simple card games help improve your memory, focus, and analytical skills.

You can even incorporate strategy into these games to spice things up. Games such as Crazy Eight or Go Fish are perfect for kids. For adults, games such as Black Jack or Poker work just as well.

Make Math Fun

Okay, math is one of the least fun things in the world, but it is also one of the best exercises to improve your logical thinking skills. It is unappealing to both adults and children, and even less so as a pastime activity. But hear us out. You see, math is more than just crunching of numbers. Those who excel in math are actually fluent in logic because the only difference between the two is numbers and letters. Math is logic simplified so everyone can make sense of it.

Thankfully, you do not need to sit and crunch numbers all evening to improve your logical thinking skills. There are plenty of fun ways to work on your math. There are plenty of mental challenges in math games on many websites or mobile phone apps that you can access.

Other math-related games such as Sudoku are also engaging and challenging, allowing you to improve your brain's ability to solve real problems faster.

Solve Mysteries and Break Codes

Another way to make learning logical thinking is by reading crime stories and detective novels. They require logical thinking from readers, after all. If reading is not your cup of tea, consider watching movies or TV shows in that genre instead. The challenge here is to solve the mystery before the hero of the story does. Of course, there will be plot twists or different interpretations of evidence, so do not be discouraged if it is actually different from what you had imagined. What matters here is you get yourself to think logically.

In this case, you often have many possibilities. Your work here is to eliminate those that are improbable or impossible. Another great brain exercise is Breaking Codes, which you can find on the internet and play with your friend.

Debate

Debates challenge us to string our thoughts together in a convincing way. While we know something is good or bad, explaining that to others is difficult. Debates force us to search for causes and consequences behind our beliefs, and turn them into strong arguments and find the logical connection behind everything.

Because you need to think logically and decide on the fly, debates can improve your logical thinking skills. So, join a debate club or organize a debate with your friends about literature, society, music, politics, etc.

Be Strategic

Logical thinking is all about understanding logical connections and putting the pieces together. By learning how to think strategically, you will develop a valuable asset for both your personal and professional life. Strategic thinking habits include anticipating, critical thinking, interpreting, deciding, and learning. You can improve this kind of thinking by playing strategic games such as board games, or video games, or design a strategy for sports events.

Notice the Pattern

Individuals with great logical thinking skills see patterns that others might otherwise miss every day. These patterns test their logical reasoning skills and how they anticipate and complete them. A great way to train pattern recognition is by scrutinizing everything and finding an answer through an educated guess.

For example, we have a string of numbers: 1, 4, 9, 16, and 25. Which of the below follows?

a. 50
b. 36
c. 44
d. 78

If you chose B, then congratulations. You noticed the pattern in the numbers. Each number in the string is squared and goes up by one. So, it's 1x1, 2x2, 3x3, 4x4, and 5x5. You need to familiarize yourself with these problems to quickly think of an answer.

7 Ways to Think More Critically

"Thinking is skilled work. It is not true that we are naturally endowed with the ability to think clearly and logically-without learning how, or without practicing" A.E. Mander.

Ask Simple Questions

Does every complicated thing need a complicated solution? Sometimes, we give too much explanation until we almost get lost or forget the original question. In order to avoid this, we will have to go back to the basic questions you asked for solving the problem. These basic questions include:

- What do you already know?
- How do you know this?
- What are you trying to prove, show, and criticize…?
- What do you miss looking at?

Question Basic Assumption

It is easy to make you look like a fool simply by not questioning your basic assumption. In the past, many scientific breakthroughs started by challenging commonly held beliefs. Those innovators in our history just looked up and said: "What if we're wrong?" If you want to make it happen in reality, you just question your assumption and think critically about what is appropriate and possible.

Know Your Mental Processes

What puts us above other animals is our ability to think. Unfortunately, thinking critically is not always easy because of the way and how we think. Our brain tends to use a mental shortcut to explain what is going on around us. The mental shortcut can be useful when you are in a situation where you have to make a quick decision such as when you are hunting large game and fighting off wild animals. However, it can be a problem when you are trying to make a decision that may affect your life. This is because these shortcuts are not always accurate. That is why it is critical to be aware of your own cognitive biases and personal prejudice as they both influence our decisions.

It is true that we as human beings have biases in our thinking, but to be aware of it is what makes critical thinking possible and something that a good critical thinker needs to take into account.

Try Reversing Things

A great way to avoid deadlock in a difficult problem is to try reversing things in a different way. It is obvious that X comes from Y, but what if Y comes from X?

A popular story that people always raise is the chicken and egg story. It is a good example to show in this case. At first, it is obvious that the chicken comes first before the egg because chickens lay eggs. However, we can also ask where the chicken comes from. It must be from somewhere. Since the chicken comes from an egg, it is true that the egg comes before the chicken, right?

Sometimes, we all know that the reverse is not true, but at least it can help you set out the right path to arrive at the best solution to the problem.

Evaluate the Existing Evidence

It is useful to review the previous work done in the past on the same topic when we are trying to solve a problem. Moreover, it is essential to evaluate the information we gain critically, or otherwise, we will reach a wrong conclusion. You can simply start by asking simple questions. For example, who collected this evidence and how did he or she do it? Why did he or she do it?

For example, one study shows that sugary cereal has health benefits. On paper, this study sounds quite persuasive. However, when you think critically and try to find out more about it, it shows that a cereal company funded the study. Thus, more or less, the company may influence the finding of the study.

However, we cannot assume automatically that the result of the study is invalid, but we have to keep in mind that we should be aware of a conflict of interest.

Remember to Think for Yourself

Some people do not trust in themselves and only rely on research or reading. They forget to think for themselves which is sometimes the most powerful tool. We should not be overconfident, but we have to understand that thinking for ourselves is really needed in responding to difficult questions. This simply happens when you are writing essays. It is so easy for most people to get lost in someone else's work that they forget to use their own thoughts, opinions, and ideas.

No One Can Think Critically 100% of the Time

It is important to understand that no one can continually think critically all the time. It is totally fine. Still, critical thinking should be employed when you need to make major decisions or solve complicated problems. However, there is no need to think critically about everything. During the decision-making process of an important decision, sometimes we will experience a lapse in our reasoning, but we just need to recognize it and try to get away from it in the future.

Ways to Improve Our Critical Thinking

Critical thinking is just the way that we process information deliberately and systematically so that we can make good decisions and understand things better.

There are some ways to think about information critically. These include:

- Conceptualizing
- Analyzing
- Synthesizing
- Evaluating

The information that we want to think of critically can come from different sources such as through:

- Observation
- Experience

- Reflection
- Reasoning
- Communication

All of these sources will guide us to believe and take action.

Critical thinking is not like how we regularly think every day. In a certain moment, we happen to think automatically, but when we think deliberately, we will use some of the critical thinking tools and skills to reach more accurate conclusions than we normally would every day.

Most of our thinking every day is not critical, and that's good for us because we do not have to spend a lot of our brain energy to think about everything. If we had to think about everything critically or deliberately, we would not have any cognitive energy left to think about something else that is more important. Thus, it is good that much of our everyday thinking happens automatically.

However, we can run into problems if we let our automatic mental process govern important decisions. If we do not have critical thinking skills, it is easy for people to control us. In our everyday life, if we fail to stop and think deliberately, it is easy for us to get caught up in pointless arguments or involved in silly things.

Chapter 6: How to Implement Critical Thinking

In this chapter, we will look at how you can implement critical thinking into your everyday life by following a few practical steps and thinking processes. Without further ado, let us get into this.

6 Steps for Effective Critical Thinking

We have to deal with problems on a day-to-day basis, from small and insignificant things to major, life-changing decisions. In many cases, we are challenged to understand a different perspective when we approach any situation. Our thought process is based on previous experience or similar situations. While that allows us to think quickly, that does not always mean we can solve problems effectively because our judgment may be clouded by our emotions. Not only that, our decisions may be further affected by prioritizing the wrong factors, or other external factors as well. Here, critical thinking allows us to establish a rational, open-minded decision-making process that is based mainly on solid facts and evidence.

As we have mentioned earlier, we have developed some mental shortcuts that help us make decisions quicker, especially during life-or-death situations. Here, critical thinking prevents us from jumping straight into conclusions. It may slow down our thought process, but it helps us in making the right decision. It helps guide us through logical steps that allow us to discover more perspectives and solutions while removing those mental shortcuts that are based on personal biases. The critical thinking process has six steps:

Knowledge

Every problem requires a clear vision to see the right solution. In this step, you need to identify the problem. To do so, ask a lot of questions to understand every little thing about the scenario. That way, you can understand what influences the outcome or what you need to address from the start. In some cases, there is no actual problem so no need to go forward with other steps. This is just as important because trying to solve a problem that does not exist is a waste of time and may worsen the situation. To identify the problem, start by asking open-ended questions to gather as much information as possible and pave the way for discussion and explore the problem. The two main questions to be asked are: What is the problem? Why do we need to solve it?

Comprehension

After identifying the situation, you can then try to understand the facts and circumstances that led up to this moment. The information gathering process should follow any of the research methods that can be changed according to the problem, the type of data available, and the deadline required to solve it.

Application

Continuing on from the previous step, this step requires you to connect the dots from the information you gathered to the resources available to solve the problem. You can use mind maps to assist you in analyzing the situation, establishing a relation between it and the core problem, and determining the best approach to proceed.

Analyze

When all the data is collected and connections have been made between it and the main issues, the situation is thoroughly assessed to identify what is really going on, the pros and cons, and the challenges involved in solving the problem. You should focus on the root causes and think of how you can address them in the solution. You can use a cause-effect diagram to help you analyze the problem and its circumstances. The diagram helps you divide the problem from its causes, identify and categorize them based on their types and impact on the problem.

Synthesis

After the problem is fully analyzed and all the relevant information is considered, the next step would be to decide how to solve the problem and create an action plan. If there is more than one solution, their advantages and drawbacks should be considered. Identify what you prioritize to find the best solution in your interest. We recommend you use SWOT analysis to identify the solution's strengths, weaknesses, opportunities, and threats.

Action

The final step is to put your decision into action. Critical thinking also applies in the action phase and the action should have its own steps. If your action plan is long-term or involves a team, it is worth having an action plan to help you execute your decision properly.

Moreover, your plan should have certain indicators to identify how well the work is going so you can evaluate your progress and adapt as needed. Of course, your action plan should be clear but flexible.

Asking the Right Questions

Critical thinking is about utilizing the information that you have to the best of your ability. As such, it is just as important to gather the right kind of information. One way to do that is either by observation or questioning. Observation can only get you so far as it can only answer some of the most basic questions.

Asking the right questions allows you to understand the situation better and analyze it properly. There are so many questions to ask, but you can follow the Star bursting method by asking the 6 questions: How, what, where, when, why, and who?

For example, suppose that you are tasked with solving an accessibility problem at your office. There have been complaints about the fact that certain stairs placement has made it difficult for disabled people to gain access to some areas, particularly the main entrance as it is slightly elevated, requiring the use of stairs. So, the questions you should ask first are:

- Who: Who is intended to use the stairs?
- What: What is wrong with the stairs? What are the options to solve the problem?
- How: How can we implement our options? How can we design the stairs in a way that disabled people can use?
- Where: Where will we use these new ideas?

- When: When do disabled people use the stairs the most?
- Why: Why do we need to change the stars' design? Why do disabled people have such a bad experience?

Alternatively, you can also use the elements of thoughts to help you identify the right questions. Elements of thoughts reflect how we think about the situation. They include purpose, questions, information, interpretation, concepts, assumptions, implications, and points of view.

- Purpose: Goals and objectives. The question: What are we trying to solve? What do I want to achieve?
- Question: Problems and issues. The question: What should I need to ask?
- Information: Data, facts, observations, experiences. The question: What do I need to know to understand the problem?

- Interpretation: Conclusions and solutions. The question: How do others come up with different solutions?
- Concepts: Definitions, theories, laws, principles, and models. The question: What is the main concept of this idea?
- Assumptions: Presuppositions and axioms. The question: What are we assuming to be true or false without confirming them?
- Implications: Results and consequences. The question: How can we implicate these new ideas?
- Point of view: Frames of reference, perspectives, orientations. The question: How are the different points of view related to the problem?

The next step, of course, is to answer all the questions without any assumptions or prejudices. Here, you should have a deep understanding of the problem and you can move forward with the steps needed to find the best solution to the problem. In our example here, the solution includes using elevators in places where disabled people can easily find and access them or using sloped platforms to allow wheelchair users to go up and down easily.

SWOT Analysis

SWOT analysis is a great tool to use, in this context, to understand the strengths, weaknesses, opportunities, and threats of a solution or situation. SWOT analysis provides a systematic way of analyzing a solution to your problem. Understanding what the pros and cons are and knowing what you should prioritize is key to identifying an optimal solution. It can be used either as an icebreaker to get people into the strategy formulation process or as a strategy tool.

Strengths

Here, you should consider both internal and external perspectives when evaluating the viability of a solution. If you have problems identifying strengths, try to make a list of the characteristics of a solution or situation. That way, you may be able to identify a few of them as strengths. Questions should include:

- What does this have that others do not?
- What advantage does the situation provide?

Weaknesses

Just like the previous element, also consider your weaknesses from both an internal and external perspective. It is best to be realistic and acknowledge any unpleasant facts as soon as possible. Be honest with yourself. Questions should include:

- What should you avoid?

- How is this solution or situation lacking?

Opportunities

A good way to analyze opportunities is to determine if their strengths open up any opportunities. If not, then look at their weaknesses and try to identify what you can get by eliminating them.

Threats

Threats mainly focus on the obstacles that hold you back from achieving your goal and evaluate how serious your weaknesses are.

Another good analysis tool called PEST analysis can help you identify opportunities and threats, ensuring that you do not overlook external factors such as government regulations or technological development.

PEST Analysis

PEST analysis is mainly used in the organizational context to help identify opportunities and threats in the business environment. For instance, you can reach new customers through new technologies, which is identified as an opportunity. On the other hand, threats can be the shrinking market, increased interest rates, or intensified competition thanks to deregulation.

PEST analysis helps you take external factors into consideration such as political, economic, socio-cultural, and technological changes in your business environment. That way, you have a better picture of the bigger forces that you are exposed to and take advantage of the opportunities that arise from them.

The difference between PEST analysis and SWOT analysis is that the former focuses on the larger factors that are often outside our domain of control such as the economy, technology, and government. The latter is a narrower scope, focusing only on the organization or individual. We recommend you use these two when you need to make major decisions as they complement each other very well.

PEST analysis comes in many names, and they are all abbreviations of what you need to consider:

- PESTLE/PESTEL: Political, economic, socio-cultural, technological, legal, and environmental
- LONGPESTLE: Local, national, and global version of PESTLE. It is best used to understand changes in a multinational organization.
- SLEPT: Socio-cultural, legal, economic, political, and technological.
- PESTLIED: Political, economic, socio-cultural, technological, legal,

international, environmental, and demographic.
- STEEPLE: Socio/Demographic, technological, economic, environmental, political, legal, and ethical.

PEST analysis has four main reasons for its use:

- It helps you identify personal or business opportunities and it helps you perceive significant threats in advance.
- It identifies the changes needed in an organization or within your business environment. It also helps you shape what you are doing so you can work to achieve the desired change rather than against it.
- It helps prevent you from starting a project that is doomed to fail for reasons outside your control.
- It can help you identify and eliminate certain assumptions that you

unconsciously make when you enter a new country, region, or market by developing an objective view of this unfamiliar environment.

Using this tool is pretty straightforward. All you need to do is brainstorm all the changes happening around you and the opportunities and threats that may come from these changes. From there, decide on which action to take.

Brainstorming

There are four main factors to consider: political, economic, socio-cultural, and technological factors.

Political Factors

Ask yourself the following questions:

- Could any pending legislation or taxation changes affect your business? If so, how?
- Are there any political factors that may change in the near future?
- What is the timescale of proposed legislative changes?
- How does the government view corporate policy, corporate social responsibility, environmental issues, and customer protection legislation? What can these factors change? Are they likely to change?
- How developed are the property rights and the rule of law?
- How widespread are corruption and organized crime?
- When is the next local, state, or national election? How can this influence government or regional policy?
- Who is the most likely winner for power? What are their views on

business policy and other policies that affect your organization?

Economic Factors

- How stable is the country's economy? Is it declining, stagnating, or growing?
- Are customers' levels of disposable income rising or falling? How likely is that to change in a few years?
- What is the unemployment rate? How easy is it to find a skilled workforce? How expensive is it to hire a skilled workforce?
- Are the exchange rates stable or do they fluctuate wildly?
- How is globalization influencing the economic environment?
- Do consumers and businesses have access to credit? If not, how will this affect your business?
- Are there any other economic factors you need to consider?

Socio-Cultural Factors

- What are the population's beliefs and lifestyle choices? How will they affect the population and your organization?
- What social attitudes and social taboos are present in that environment? How could they affect your business? Have there been any socio-cultural changes that affect this?
- What employment patterns, attitudes toward work, and job market trends can you identify? Are they different for different age groups?
- What is the population's growth rate and age profile? How likely is it to change?
- What are society's levels of social mobility, education, and health? Are they changing? How? What impact do they have?
- Will generation shifts in attitude affect your business?

Technological Factors

- Are there any new technologies you can use to boost your organization's performance?
- Are there any new upcoming technologies that can affect the business environment?
- Do your competitors have access to new technologies that can give them an advantage?
- In which areas do government and educational institutions focus their research? How can you take advantage of this?
- Are there any existing technological hubs you can work with or learn from?
- How have infrastructure changes affected your work patterns such as levels of remote working?
- Are there any other technological factors you should be aware of?

Opportunities

From the extensive list of what you have gathered from the previous PEST analysis, you can then proceed to study each change and how it can pave the way for new opportunities for you. For instance, can it help you develop new products, assess new markets, or make the production process more efficient?

Threats

It is just as important to understand how the changes can negatively affect your business. If you identify the threats early enough, you may be able to avoid them or at least minimize their impact.

For instance, if a new piece of technology is threatening your business, what can you do about it to improve the product instead? If your target market is in demographic decline, what other areas of the market can you access?

Action

Finally, after identifying major opportunities and threats, establishing an action plan to exploit opportunities and manage or eliminate risks, can then put your plans into action. As always, make sure your plan is not too rigid. You need to establish indicators to tell how well you are doing. If things are not going well, then you should be able to identify what went wrong and how you can change your plan. Evaluate, rinse, and repeat.

The Six Thinking Hats

Your thinking style has its own pros and cons. Optimistic thinkers often see the chances but tend to overlook the risks or downsides associated with them. Cautious thinkers are the opposite, seeing only risks and not opportunities. By changing up your thinking style, you may be able to find new solutions to tricky problems.

The best way to approach a problem is by viewing it from various angles. You can use the "Six Thinking Hats" model to help you adopt different viewpoints. It can also be used as a decision-checking tool in group situations because you can encourage everyone to explore the situation from many perspectives simultaneously.

By forcing you to move away from your habitual style of thinking, the Six Thinking Hats model allows you to look at a situation from a different perspective, allowing you to view a situation more objectively.

While you can think up a good solution to your problem using a rational, positive viewpoint, it is still worth exploring the problem from other angles. For instance, you can view the problem from an intuitive, creative, emotional, or risk management viewpoint. You may be surprised to see what good solutions you are missing out on. Plus, not deciding these can mean making a decision that is poorly received by others because their needs are not met, creative ideas are not used, or essential contingency plans are not acknowledged.

How to Implement the Six Thinking Hats Model

The Six Thinking Hats model can be used in meetings by assigning everyone to every hat evenly, or on your own. In a meeting, it has the added benefit of confrontation prevention because when everyone is viewing the problem from different angles, all their opinions are valid. As you may have already guessed, each thinking hat is a way of thinking.

White Hat

White Hat is a thinking style that primarily focuses on the available data. You look at what information you have, analyze past trends, and try to spot a pattern or learn something from it. Try to find gaps in your knowledge and try to account for them or fill them. It is important that you do not proceed further than comprehending the facts and knowledge gap. The questions here are: "What do we know?" and "What is the data that we have?"

Red Hat

Red hat focuses more on intuition, gut feeling, and emotion. Think of this for you and those affected by your decisions. Most importantly, try to understand the responses coming from those who do not understand your reasoning. The objective of this thinking style is to understand the emotional reaction from everyone but not try to understand the reason behind those reactions. Here, you should ask "What do you feel about this suggestion?" and "Does anything feel off to you?"

Black Hat

Black hat thinking focuses mainly on the negative outcomes of any decision. Wearing this hat, you need to look at everything cautiously and defensively. Instead of seeing how it could work, see where it could go wrong. This is critical as it highlights any weak points in a plan, allowing you to eliminate, alter, or prepare contingency plans to counter them.

This style of thinking helps you build a more solid plan because you spot fatal flaws and risks before you implement the plan, which would be too late by then as you may have already sunk resources into it. Many successful people are often over-optimistic about their situation, which tends to leave them vulnerable as they cannot see problems in advance. This makes them unprepared for difficulties. You should ask the following questions: "What are the risks?" and "How can this go wrong?"

Yellow Hat

This is a positive way of thinking. The yellow represents hope as it is the color of the sun. You adopt an optimistic viewpoint to help you discover all the benefits of your decisions and the values in them. Yellow Hat thinking often serves to motivate you when the going gets tough. The questions to be asked here are: "What are the advantages of implementing this solution?" and "Why do you think this is viable?"

Green Hat

The color green represents intelligence. In this context, it represents creativity. Wearing this hat, you need to think of creative approaches to a problem. This is a free way of thinking where there is little criticism of ideas.

Blue Hat

This style of thinking focuses mainly on process control. It is intended to guide the whole decision-making process and determine which thinking that everyone should use. For instance, when ideas are running dry, they may focus on Green Hat thinking. When things go wrong and contingency plans are needed, Black Hat thinking will be used.

An Example of Six Hats

So, how do these go together in a real-life situation? All of them can be applied to different scenarios based on the aim of the decision. Moreover, you can also use this thinking model in an educational context to help students develop creative thinking skills and learn how to identify solutions based on an in-depth understanding of the problems. We have two examples for you. In the first example, different people wear different Thinking Hats. In the second example, everyone wears the same Thinking Hat and then changes throughout the decision-making process.

Example 1: Suppose that you are one of the directors of a property company. The board of directors is considering whether they should build a new office block. From a glance, everyone can tell that the economy is flourishing and there is a high demand for vacant office spaces as they are being bought left, right, and center. So, how does the Six Thinking Hat model fit into the decision-making process?

Starting with the White Hat, everyone looks at the data they have. They see that their supply, which is vacant office space in the city, is going down. If they decide to build a new office building now, the existing office space should be in extremely short supply by the time the new building block is finished. You also know that the economy is growing and steady growth is expected to continue.

Then, thinking with the Red Hat, some directors may say that the current building design looks gloomy and old. They may say that people may find the working environment unappealing from the design and want it changed.

Looking at the Black Hat thinkers, they ponder whether the economic forecast may be wrong. If the economy were to suddenly experience a downturn, many office buildings would sit empty or only partly occupied for a long time. Suddenly, the company is looking at an economy with high supply and low demand. Not only that, the Red Hat thinkers point out the aesthetic flaw of the office design, so other companies will only buy office buildings that are more attractive.

On the other spectrum, the Yellow Hat thinkers know that there are risks associated with investing in the construction of another office building block. They point out that, suppose the economy is still doing well and their projections are correct, then they have much to gain as the company can make a hearty profit. Even if they were to suffer an economic downturn, perhaps they could sell their buildings before then, or rent them out on long-term leases that could last through any recession, which makes purchasing their buildings an appealing prospect for many businesses even if the buildings themselves are not as pleasing to the eyes.

The Green Hat thinkers took the advice from the Red Hat, Yellow Hat, and Black Hat thinkers and consider whether they should redesign the building to make it more appealing. They have a few options to consider here. They can either build prestige offices that people would want to rent regardless of the economic climate. They can also wait until the economic downturn happens, which would drive down office building costs. Then, they can invest the money into buying those properties, selling them after the economy is flourishing again.

Finally, the Blue Hat thinkers control the whole process, ensuring that the discussion and ideas continue to flow as well as encouraging other directors to change their thinking hats to get as many ideas as possible. With these thinking styles put together, the committee of directors has a much clearer picture of the situation and its possible outcomes and is able to make decisions accordingly.

Example 2: This time, you are in a group of designers who are tasked to redesign your company's product package. The flow would then be something like this:

First, everyone puts on the White Thinking Hat to discuss what they know about the package. What does it look like? How do our competitors design their packages? What do the customers say about our package? How well-received is that of our competitors?

Then, everyone proceeds to the Yellow Thinking Hat and identifies the advantages of redesigning the package, its process, and what the product can benefit from the new design. So, you can ask about the benefits of the redesign or what positive impact the new design brings.

From there, the whole team puts on the Black Thinking Hat and looks at the disadvantage of the design change. They discuss the negative impacts on product sales and marketing targets. Here, everyone looks at the risks associated with the design change.

Everyone then proceeds to the Red Thinking Hat, reflecting their emotional reactions toward the current package and the new one. How does everyone feel about the current package? How does it compare to the new one? What do the customers feel about the new design? How does the team feel about changing the current design?

In the Green Hat thinking phase, everyone starts to think of the new design from a creative and innovative perspective. This helps the team think about the new design and how they can improve upon the previous one by looking at its design flaws.

Throughout the entire decision-making process, the moderators wear the Blue Hat to keep the ideas and discussions going and direct them in a way that facilitates the session.

As you can see, the Six Thinking Hats model allows us to view a situation from various standpoints, giving us the chance to further analyze the situation to gain an in-depth understanding. Moreover, this model also provides us with a systematic thinking method by covering the topic from different approaches. This kind of organized thinking can lead you to an ideal solution in the decision-making process.

The Paul-Elder Critical Thinking Framework

Back in 2002, Paul and Elder introduced a new critical thinking framework to assist students to sharpen their critical thinking skills by identifying thinking parts and evaluating their usage. The goal of this framework aims to improve our reasoning by identifying its different elements by looking at three main elements: reasoning, intellectual standards, and intellectual traits.

Elements of Reasoning

We use different thinking types to understand an issue. Even in our Six Thinking Hats model, they all have eight common elements. This is similar to the elements of thoughts we have discussed previously. Here, we look at:

- Purpose: Defining a goal or objective such as solving a problem or achieving a target.
- Attempt: What is the previous experience to solve a similar problem?
- Assumption: Before we proceed to solve the problem, we may know little about it. So, we can use assumptions as the basis of our research. Normally, we start with inductive assumptions and then conduct additional research to validate these assumptions.
- Point of view: We look at our thinking styles here. The Six Thinking Hats model is a good example.
- Data, information, and evidence: This covers all the information related to the issue we are trying to solve.

- Concept and ideas: This covers principles, models, and theories related to the topic.
- Inferences and interpretations: This is how we conclude solutions based on all the previous parts.
- Implications and consequences: Every reason should lead to consequences that result from the implementation of the reasoning process.

Intellectual Standards

Reasoning elements need to have a good standard to achieve their purpose and ensure the accuracy of results. There are nine factors you can use to determine whether the parts above are of good quality. They include clarity, accuracy, precision, relevance, depth, breadth, logic, significance, and fairness. To evaluate the parts, you can ask a few questions based on these factors:

- Clarity:
    - Can you explain?
    - Can you give me an example?
    - Can you illustrate what you mean?
- Accuracy:
    - How can we verify that?
    - How can we determine if this is true?
    - How can we test that?
- Precision:
    - Can you be more specific?
    - Can you tell me more about it?
    - Can you be more exact?
- Relevance:
    - How is this related to the problem?
    - How can this help us with the issue?
    - How does that connect to the question?
- Depth:

- What makes this difficult?
    - What are the difficulties we need to deal with?
    - What are the complexities of this problem?
- Breadth:
    - Is there a need to look at this problem from another angle?
    - Do we need to consider another point of view?
    - Should we look at this problem in other ways?
- Logic:
    - Does this make sense together?
    - Is the flow of ideas logical?
    - Does the evidence support the claim?
- Significance:
    - Is this the most important problem to consider?
    - Is this what we need to focus on?

- - Which of these things are the most important?
- Fairness:
  - Is my thinking justifiable in this context?
  - Did I consider what others think?
  - Is my purpose fair given the situation?

Intellectual Traits

After applying all of the reasoning elements and verifying them using intellectual standards, you should expect the following to be developed:

Humility

You know the limitations and the circumstances that may cause biases and self-deceptivity. It depends on whether you recognize that people only claim what they actually know.

Courage

Courage here means that you can now address ideas fairly regardless of your personal biases or emotions against their points of view. It helps us develop our ability to evaluate ideas despite our perceptions and presumptions against it.

Empathy

Empathy is all about developing the ability to see the world through another person's point of view to understand them. Moreover, it demonstrates how others have arrived at their conclusions so that we may be able to enhance our understanding of the problem at hand.

Integrity

This part is related to developing one's ability to combine with the reasoning of others and avoid confusion of our own reasoning. Integrity focuses more on the ability to comprehend others' reasoning of the topic and integrate it to solve the problem effectively.

Perseverance

This trait focuses on facing the truth of the situation in spite of all the difficulties or other unpleasant information you have to take in such as difficulties, frustration, and obstacles. This allows you to build more rational reasoning and prepare for difficulties as they happen.

Confidence in Reason

When you apply the reasoning elements and encourage people to come up with their own reasons behind their understanding, they build confidence in their reasoning and think in a more rational way.

Fair-Mindedness

This trait develops your ability to look objectively at everything without interfering with your emotions, interests, or biases.

With all of these three key components combined, we can understand our thought process better and know how to evaluate our own reasoning systematically. The Paul-Elder critical framework allows you to analyze your own thought patterns and work to improve them.

The Ultimate Guide to Critical Thinking

Developing and improving critical thinking skills is considered a life study and it is a skill that is worth improving on and pursuing in life. For most educators, critical thinking skills are believed to be one of the most essential skills for life beyond school education. Learning how to think critically is not easy, but it is something that we can improve and learn. If critical thinking was easy, everyone would have the ability to do so. However, it is still the most important skill we need to have in life. We are all aware of the universal concept that there are a lot of definitions, views, and opinions on what critical thinking really is.

We will provide you with tools and resources to be able to reflect independently on the exploration of critical thinking and you can define critical thinking for yourself. You will also be able to develop this skill in yourself, in children, and other people.

We have collected some definitions of critical thinking from other websites that discuss the meaning of critical thinking:

According to the Foundation for Critical Thinking, Critical thinking is the intellectually disciplined process of actively and skillfully conceptualizing, applying, analyzing, synthesizing, and/or evaluating information gathered from, or generated by, observation, experience, reflection, reasoning or communication as a guide to belief and action.

The Stanford Encyclopedia of Philosophy pointed out that critical thinking is a widely accepted educational goal. While the exact definition is highly debatable, they all share a common concept: careful thinking directed to a goal.

Richard W. Paul said critical thinking is thinking about what you are thinking as you are thinking so as to improve your thinking.

Grant Wiggins also said that thoughtful people think about what they learn and the result of what they do. They take all the assumptions and implications of ideas and actions to the table, examine them, and challenge them if needed.

For us, what we define as critical thinking is all about clear, rational, logical, and independent thinking. In order to improve critical thinking, we have to improve the way we think by analyzing, evaluating, and reconstructing. Critical thinking is also about the self-regulated and self-corrective manner in the way we think. Critical thinking also involves communication and problem-solving skills, and we definitely have to avoid any form of bias or what we call egocentric tendencies. We can think critically to apply it in any kind of situation or problem you want to solve.

Developing Critical Thinking

We have already learned what critical thinking is and why it is important, so now it is time to learn about how we can develop and build critical thinking skills. According to Wabi-sabi Learning, they have developed a number of useful resources that we can use to develop critical thinking skills. These include:

Critical Thinking Skills Cheatsheet: it consists of questions that you can use to exercise your critical thinking skills whenever you want to discuss new information. These questions can be broadly applied in many situations. These questions are Wh-questions.

The following is the ultimate cheat sheet for critical thinking from Wabisabi Learning

WHO
Who benefits from this?
Who have you also heard discuss this?
Who is this harmful to?
Who would be the best person to consult?
Who makes decisions about this?
Who will be the key people in this?
Who is most directly affected?
Who deserves recognition for this?

WHAT
What are the strengths/weaknesses?

What is the best/worst case scenario?
What is another perspective?
What is most/least important?
What is another alternative?
What can we do to make a positive change?
What would be a counter-argument?
What is getting in the way of our actions?

WHERE
Where would we see this in the real world?
Where can we get more information?
Where are there similar concepts/situations?
Where do we go for help with this?
Where is there the most need for this?
Where will this idea take us?
Where in the world would this be a problem?
Where are the areas for improvement?

WHEN

When is this accepted/unaccepted?

When will we know we've succeeded?

When would this benefit our society?

When has this played a part in our history?

When would this cause a problem?

When can we expect this to change?

When is the best time to take action?

When should we ask for help with this?

WHY

Why is this problem/challenge?

Why should people know about this?

Why is it relevant to me/others?

Why has it been this way for so long?

Why is this the best/worst scenario?

Why have we allowed this to happen?

Why are people influenced by this?

Why is there a need for this today?

HOW

How is this similar to_____?

How does this benefit us/others?
How does this disrupt things?
How does this harm us/others?
How do we know the truth about this?
How do we see this in the future?
How will we approach this safely?
How can we change this for our good?

5 Steps to Asking Good Questions

Critical Thinking Questions

Critical thinking is all about questions. We need to ask questions in order to find out more information related to our problems. Asking questions is a skill that we can practice every day. Asking questions plays a very significant role in developing critical thinking. If we ask good and the right questions, we will receive useful and right answers that we can use to solve the problem.

The foundation of learning, living, and of course, critical thinking is asking good questions. It is believed that much of our success comes from asking good and right questions. Asking good questions can prepare you for the right path to follow in both study and critical thinking. We will show you how you can really do it. It is a simple process from Wabisabi Learning.

Focus:
What do I want to know exactly?
What information am I missing?
Is this more than a simple Yes or NO question?
Am I going for deeper knowledge?

Purpose:
Why am I asking this?
Do I want to gather facts or opinions?
Do I need simple clarification?
Do I want to offer a different perspective?

Intent:

How do I want people to respond?

Do I want the answer that is useful to others?

Do I want to start an argument or open a discussion?

Is the question superficial and not really useful or important?

Am I asking out of frustration or curiosity?

Do I really care about the answer?

Am I willing to show respect/deference to the person I am asking?

Framing:

Am I using easily understandable terms and working?

Is my question neutral or does it contain bias or opinion?

Is it too long or too short?

Does it contain the focus of what I want to know?

Does the question focus on only one thing?

Is it muddled with other inquiries that don't belong?

Am I using easy words to make my questions understandable?

Is my question neutral or does it have any bias or opinion?

Is it too long or too short?

Does it lead to the answer I want?

Does it focus on only one thing?

Did I go off the tangents with my line of questioning?

Follow-up:

Do I have any more questions I should ask? What else did I miss?

Will the person be available to answer my question?

If I still am not satisfied with the answer, what then?

What can I do if I still don't understand?

Other than that, there are games and activities that you can do to engage your critical thinking on multiple levels. We can use the following critical thinking games to develop teamwork skill and collaborative ability.

We have got some stories and scenarios that are based on ethics and morality from Wabisabi Learning that we can use to think critically.

Tom found an expensive phone in the school hallway. There is no way to tell whom it belongs to and it is not near anyone's locker:
Should he
1. Give it to lost and found
2. Ask if it belongs to anyone there
3. Keep it and not say anything

Cade's friend is worried about an upcoming test. If she flunks it, she will fail the entire semester and be unable to graduate with Cade and her other friends. Cade took the test previously, got 100%, and remembers all the answers.

Should she
1. Tell her friend the answers
2. Offer to coach her friend
3. Not get involved at all

Hank overhears two students boasting about how they posted inappropriate pictures of female students online just to get a laugh. He is friends with them, but he knows that this is not the first time they have done something like this.

Should he
1. Mind his own business
2. Report the incident to the school principal
3. Confront the boys and defend the student

You witness a bank robbery and follow the criminal down an alleyway. He stops at an orphanage and gives them all the money.

Would you

1. Report the man to police since he committed a crime
2. Leave him alone because you saw him do a good deed

An old friend of yours tells you that he or she has received death threats online. They also mentioned that the messages have been relentless, which prevents them from focusing. They are too afraid and this has affected their grades. You know of a few people who may be behind this.

Would you
1. Tell your friend just to ignore them
2. Encourage them to report the abuse
3. Risk confronting the ones you suspect

Chapter 7: Common Critical Thinking Pitfalls and How to Avoid Them

In this chapter, we will discuss some of the most common critical thinking mistakes and manipulations that people use to sway opinions and alter the truth. Before we get into that, let us go back to the basics and understand critical thinking a bit more.

Three Basic Building Blocks of Critical Thinking

The three basics of critical thinking: Claims, Issues, and Arguments

These are the three basic building blocks of critical thinking; claim, issues and arguments and critical thinking is all about these three elements. We have to be able to identify, separate, and analyze these three elements.

Claim

In the previous paragraph, we have already mentioned the claim. Claim is one of the three basic elements in critical thinking. Claims are what we say aloud or write down. We use it to convey information and express our beliefs and opinions. This is the primary use of a claim. Claims can also be statements that can be true or false. For example, Alaska is the biggest state in America. It is a true claim. Another example, Alaska is the most populous state in America. This is a false claim as Alaska is not the most populous state in America. There is life living on other planets. This is either true or false as we do not know yet which planet. Again, this is the main role of critical thinking, which is to examine and evaluate the claims being made including their relationships to each other. It is a principal task of critical thinking.

The claim that we are discussing here can be about anything - from small and modest interests or earth-shaking ones. Claims about whether water can help whiten your skin, whether beer can make you fat, whether the president should step down or that war will take place; everything is fair game.

There are many claims that require little or no critical evaluation. They are just obviously true or false that no one has a doubt or needs any critical examination. This can be, for example, whether a shop nearby is still open requires only a phone call and not an investigation. However, there are still a lot of claims that require a close look and examination. It can be a claim about your personal decisions. For example, should you propose marriage to a girl whom you just saw at the corner of the street? It can also be social matters; for example, should we have a capital penalty for rapists? Moreover, if you hold an important position and have to make a decision that will affect other people, it requires you to have a careful examination and evaluation on the claim.

Issues

This is the most important part of the matter. When we want to turn a claim into a question and when we want to know the truth or falsity of the claim, this is where the issue comes up. Claims turned into issues and supported by arguments are the main point of critical thinking. The issue has a very simple concept as it is described as nothing more than a question. Sometimes, we can use both words interchangeably. What is the question? The question is simply raised in order to know whether or not the given claim is true.

Here are two ways that we can use to state an issue:

1. By asking a question, is John taller than Mark?
2. Whether John is taller than Mark.

When we can answer either one of the two questions, the answer will determine whether the claim "John is taller than Mark" is true.

Another example is Singaporean lawmakers do not like the recent fashion of young people who have dyed their hair red, and they want to make a law that states it is illegal to have red hair. Then, in parliament, the claim "it should be illegal to have red hair" was under consideration or we can say: Whether it should be illegal to have red hair was the issue before the Singaporean lawmakers. It is important to remember that when we think about a claim critically, we turn it into a question and make it an issue.

Sometimes, there is no point for you to consider an argument for or against a claim if you do not have any idea what would be needed toward it being true or false. That means you cannot find any evidence to support your claim in order to say that the claim is true or false. We really have no idea how to argue or support the claim. For instance, there is no one identical to you who lives in a different dimension.

This does not mean that it is worth only discussing the claims that can be proven by scientific or experimental methods. Sometimes, claims are made in contexts which are not really important to know whether the claim is true or not. For example, people tell you a joke. Even though the truth is really necessary, scientific methods are not necessarily needed to prove it. The same way in mathematics, the mathematical theory is not confirmed by experimentation but rather the deduction from other mathematical hypothesis. Some people believe that if the proof is revealed in the Bible, it means it is a true claim. Therefore, you have to have some ideas about what is needed to be used for and against a claim's truth if you are really serious about finding the truth about a claim.

Arguments

We have already identified what the claim is, and the issue is. Now, let's move to another one which is about argument to weigh the reason for and against the claim with an attempt to determine the truth and falsity of the claim. This is where argument comes into play. Argument is one of the three basic building blocks of critical thinking and it is the most essential ingredient in critical thinking. At the core of an argument, it is a bit difficult to understand, but to put simply, we produce an argument when we want to give a reason for thinking that the claim is true. For example, there is an issue happening with Smith. We will take a look at whether Smith should be excused for being absent from the class. Smith speaks with his teacher. "My mother passed away and I had to skip class in order to attend the funeral." So here, Smith has offered a reason for thinking he should be excused for being absent from the class, so he has made an argument. For now, let's keep it simple, there are a couple more terms that are used in talking about arguments. A claim given as a reason for believing in another claim is a premise. The claim that the premise should give a reason is called a conclusion of the argument. To make it clear, the issue is "whether Smith should be excused for being absent from the class" or another way if you want to change is "Should Smith be excused for being absent from class?"

Premise: Smith's mother passed away and he had to skip class to attend the funeral.

Conclusion: Smith should be excused for being absent from the class.

The role of the conclusion here is to answer the question asked by the issue. The conclusion states a position on the issue.

There are two components to the premise's support of the conclusion. First, the premise can be used to support the conclusion only if the premise is true. In order to see the truth of the premise, we then need to do an independent investigation and we also need more arguments in order to support this claim. Second, the premise that is going to support the conclusion should be relevant to the conclusion. It can sometimes be called Cogent. The two requirements above will indeed show that if the premise, if true, must actually bear on the truth of the conclusion, then it will really increase the likelihood that the conclusion is true.

An argument comprises of two parts. One is the premise or premises, and it will tell us the reason for thinking that the conclusion is true.

What Arguments Are Not

In critical thinking, when we use the word "argument," we are not talking about two people having a feud about something. It is important to remember that we do not even need two people. We can use arguments in our own critical thinking all the time.

It is also important to understand that not everything that looks like an argument is an argument. Sometimes, it is nothing more than just a fact.

For instance, there are 5 thieves in a bank robbery, and more people have learned how easy it is to get into a bank where there are lots of people. The local police department reminds all banks in the city to keep a close watch and strengthen their security.

Even though these statements are related to each other by talking about the same topic, none of them acts as a reason for believing the other and, therefore, there is no argument.

Another different example: the number of people who have learned to hack bank accounts has increased in the past year, so you are more likely to be the victim of this scam now than you were a year ago.

So here, the first claim gives support for believing the second claim. We have an argument in the sentence that shows the reason why we are more likely to be the victim of this scam now than you were a year ago.

Arguments and Explanations

There are a lot of words that often confuse people about arguments such as rhetorical flourishes, asides, tangents, jokes. We need to go through all of these things before arriving at the actual argument. In addition, an argument can also be confused with two common kinds of things, which are explanations and persuasion.

Basically, the role of an argument is to offer support or to prove a conclusion, while an explanation tells us more about what caused something, how something happened, how it works or what it is made out of and so on. For instance, you argued that a dog has a bad smell. This is an argument about a dog, and you want to know why the dog has a bad smell. Then, we need an explanation. Another example, domestic violence has increased over the past few years, an argument, while to know why domestic violence has increased over the past few years is an explanation. Argument and explanation are two completely different things and they always confuse people easily.

Argument and Persuasions

Some people define an argument as an attempt to convince someone of something. This is not right. The role of an argument is to support and prove a conclusion. When you want to win someone over with your opinion, you will try to persuade them and argue. It is true that you may use argument when you want to persuade someone of something, but not all of those arguments used to persuade and attempt to persuade involve argument. It is the fact that giving arguments is not the most effective way of convincing people.

Two Kinds of Good Arguments

There are two good arguments, which are good deductive and good inductive arguments.

Deductive arguments

It is the first type of good argument, a good deductive argument. If a good deductive argument is valid, it is not possible for the premises to be true and the conclusion false.

Premise: Sam lives in Tokyo.
Conclusion: Therefore, Sam lives in Japan.

This is a valid argument because it is not possible that Sam lives in Tokyo and he does not live in Japan.

Another example,
Premise: Mark is taller than his girlfriend and his girlfriend is taller than her mother.
Conclusion: Therefore, Mark is taller than his girlfriend's mother.

This is also a valid argument because it is not possible for Mark to be taller than his girlfriend and not taller than his girlfriend's mother.

In short, the premises of a good deductive argument, assuming they are true, will surely prove or support the conclusion.

Inductive Argument

The premise of a good inductive argument does not prove or demonstrate the conclusion but just supports it. It only raises the probability of being true to the conclusion.

Premise: Alex lives in Belgium.
Conclusion: Therefore, he loves drinking beer.

In this example, Alex lives in Belgium, and it is more probable that he loves drinking beer.

The Language of Arguments

Besides the word "therefore," there are other words that work the same way to show the conclusion. These include

- It follows that...
- This shows that...
- Thus...
- Hence...
- Consequently...
- Accordingly...
- So...
- My conclusion is...

All of these words and phrases have been used everywhere not only as a conclusion indicator, but we always assume that what follows them is a conclusion of an argument.

We also have words that show the premise to be stated:
- Since...
- For...
- Because...
- In view of ...
- This is implied by...

- Given...

Once again, some arguments do not consist of any words indicating a conclusion, and we have to pay attention to whether the statement is going to support or demonstrate something.

Vagueness

Vagueness, perhaps, is the most common form of unclear thinking or writing. When a word or a group of words is vague, it has an unclear meaning. It is not clear at all for us to understand, interpret, and express. It contains a vague meaning that requires more than just simple reading to understand.

Vagueness plays a very significant role in our legal system. In law, we have to deal with vagueness carefully. Otherwise, it will have many different interpretations in its meaning from various people when we want to apply it in a real situation.

Ambiguity

A word, phrase, or sentence that is said to be ambiguous contains more than one meaning. For instance, does "John cashed a check" mean that he gave cash to somebody or somebody gave cash to him? "Sophic is renting her apartment" can mean she is renting her apartment to someone or she is renting her apartment from someone.

Most of the time, the interpretation that a speaker or writer wants to make for a claim is obvious, but the ambiguity can still happen and its consequences will not just make you smile.

Semantic Ambiguity

One claim can have several ways of ambiguity, but the most common one is that a claim contains an ambiguous word or phrase that can lead to what we call "Semantic ambiguity."

Grouping Ambiguity

It is actually a kind of semantic ambiguity that is not clear whether the claim refers to the whole group collectively or each individual member of the group. For example, teachers make more money than doctors.

This example is true if it refers to teachers and doctors collectively because there are more teachers than doctors. However, it is obvious that the example is false if it refers to individual doctors and teachers. It is not different from other ambiguities that can affect the way we think about the claim as it may interfere with our thinking.

Syntactic Ambiguity

Syntactic ambiguity happens when there are more interpretations on the claim due to its structures, or the construction of the words in the claim that can give the wrong meaning of the claim. Sometimes, we can call it grammatical ambiguity as it involves the grammatical structure of the sentence. For example, the chicken is ready to eat. Now, let's consider this statement. This statement can express two meanings if we do not analyze it correctly. Firstly, it can mean that the chicken is ready for feeding or needs something to eat. Secondly, it can also mean that the chicken is already cooked and ready for us to eat.

The Claim and its Sources

There are two things that we can use to evaluate credibility. The first thing is the claims themselves, and the second thing is the claims' sources. If we are told that a dog can fly in the air, we will dismiss this claim immediately because such a claim already has no credibility no matter where it is from. It is so obvious that the claim has no credibility and we must not believe it. However, if we are told that ducks mate for life, it is a credible claim, but we need to find the source of the claim to know whether to believe it or not. Moreover, if we can find the information related to this claim in a bird book or research from an expert, we are more likely to believe in the claim.

Evaluating the Content of the Claim

Some claims express their own true meaning within the claims themselves, and we tend to believe in them regardless of who made them or where they came from. It is so obvious that it is a credible claim. However, when a claim does not stand up to its meaning, it is because the claim is in conflict with either our own observation or background knowledge.

Personal Observation

Personal observation is one of the most reliable sources of information in the world. Therefore, it is reasonable to feel doubt about any claims that have a direct conflict with what we have observed. For example, you have just come from the home of John, a mutual friend of yours and David's, and you have seen his new black Range Rover vehicle. You meet

David and he tells you that John has just bought a new Range Rover vehicle, a red one. In this case, you do not need to have critical thinking skills to reject David's claim because it is so obvious that the claim is in direct conflict with what you just observed when you were in John's home.

Factors that Influence Our Observation

Our observations can be influenced by several factors and our recollection of them. The factors influencing can be from a physical condition such as bad lighting, lots of noise, the speed of the event, and more. It is also crucial to keep in mind that people are not equally created when it comes to making an observation. Our hope, beliefs, fears, and expectations can also affect our observation. If you tell someone that your house is like a home of rats, they are more likely to believe it if they see the evidence of rats. Moreover, our personal biases and interests are other factors that can affect our perception and judgment.

Sometimes, we may not look at the selfishness and greediness of the people we like or love, and if we are inspired by someone, everything that that person does seems to be amazing. Naturally, people who we do not like can hardly do anything that we don't think is selfish and self-centered. If we want to be successful in doing a project, we need to see more evidence for success than is actually presented. In addition, if we want to see a project fail, we tend to exaggerate the flaws that we see in it and imagine that we do not see any problem in the project at all.

Background Knowledge

We can have background knowledge by learning from our own observation and from others. The word background implies the information we learned sometime in the past and we cannot specify where or when we learned this information. Most of our background information is well confirmed by a variety of sources and we will dismiss any claims that are in conflict with the store of background information even if we cannot prove it wrong through direct observation. "Mango trees grow in abundance in the North Pole" we will reject this claim immediately even if we are not supposed to confirm or reject the statement by direct observation. When we first encounter such a claim, we have to treat the claim by making a rough assessment of how credible the claim seems to us. We assess the claim by using our background knowledge or information to see the consistency of the claim-like how likely it is to be true with that claim or information. If the claim is consistent with our background knowledge, we will give the claim some degree of credibility. However, if it is in conflict with our background knowledge or information, we will give the claim a low degree of credibility or reject the claim if there is no further evidence to be shown or proved.

Fallacy

Fallacies are shortcomings that can affect or weaken your argument, and make your argument less effective. The idea of fallacy is to argue that someone holds views that are not really what other people believe. You will be able to be good at evaluating the arguments you read and hear if you can find them on your own and in others' writing. There are two things that you have to keep in mind in fallacy. The first is that fallacious arguments happen very often and are quite convincing, at least to people who are weak in critical thinking. You usually see a lot of fallacious arguments in magazines, newspapers, and other sources. The second one is that, sometimes, it is quite difficult to tell if the argument being made is truly fallacious. You can be told a weak, somewhat weak, somewhat strong and/or very strong argument. An argument that has several parts may contain some strong sections and some weak ones. In this section, we will help you look critically at your own arguments and move them away from the weak to the strong ones.

Types of Fallacy

For all of the following points, we will explain, and give an example on how you avoid fallacies in your own arguments.

Hasty Generalization

Hasty generalization involves making the assumption about a group of things or people based on a small or little sample, and usually, the sample is not adequate enough to make that assumption.

Example: "My colleague told me that mathematics class is very difficult and I also had that expcrience too." All mathematics classes are difficult. By using these two opinions, we cannot make a general assumption that all mathematics classes are difficult. It is just not enough to come up with this conclusion.

In order to avoid this fallacy, you need to look at the kind of sample you are using. Did you come to this conclusion based on your own experience in a few situations? Did you just rely on the views and experiences of a few people? In this case, you need to ask yourself whether further evidence and information is needed to make a conclusion. Exactly. You will have to have more evidence to make a conclusion about mathematics classes in this case.

Appeal to Authority

When we want other people to believe what we are trying to claim, we often tend to refer to our respected sources or authorities and explain their role or position in the issue we are discussing. If we want to get our readers or listeners to totally agree with us by giving them a famous name or appealing to an authority who is not really an expert in this field, we are trying to make an appeal-to-authority fallacy.

For example, the death penalty should be removed. Many famous and respected people, such as singer Guy Handsome, have expressed their opinion against this law.

In this case, singer Guy Handsome is included as an authority who is believed to be respected in order to make people follow the claim. The point is we should not follow any claims just because it contains someone famous or respected in the claim without thinking about it critically.

There are two ways that you can use to avoid committing appeal to authority. First, we have to make sure that the authority we rely on has to be an expert on the subject we are discussing. Second, not just because "Dr. Authority believes XXX" so we should believe

XXX too." What we should do is try to explain the reasoning or evidence that shows how the authority used to arrive at his/her opinion. The authority's reputation is not more important than the source and evidence of his/her opinion.

Appeal to Pity

This appeal will take place when an arguer wants you to agree or believe in his/her claim by making you feel sorry for someone.

For example, "I understand that the exam is graded based on my performance, but you should give me good scores. I have been sick for the past several days, and my motorbike is broken, so I didn't have enough time to study."

The conclusion from the arguer is "You should give good scores," but the requirement for getting good scores is based on learning. The arguer wants us to accept that people who have a hard week deserve good scores; which is unacceptable. The information given by the arguer to get us to agree with it is not logically relevant. As a result, the argument is fallacious.

The thing to remember in order to avoid committing appeal to pity is to make sure that you are trying to get your audience to agree with you by making them feel sorry for you or someone.

Appeal to Ignorance

For an appeal to ignorance, the arguer basically tries to say that "There is no conclusive evidence on the issue at hand." Therefore, you should believe my claim for this reason.

For example, "For centuries, people have been trying to prove that God does exist, but no one has been able to prove it. Therefore, God does not exist." There is also a different claim about God. "For centuries, people have been trying to prove that God does not exist, but no one has been able to prove it yet. Therefore, God does exist." For these two claims, the arguers are trying to make the conclusion true just because of the lack of explanation and evidence to prove at the present time.

In order to avoid committing appeal to ignorance, you should closely observe the arguments that have no evidence and then come up with a conclusion from the lack of evidence.

Ad Hominem and tuquoque

These two types of fallacy focus on the person who makes the claim rather than the quality of the claim itself. The word Ad Hominem means "against the person" and tuquoque means "you too." In these two fallacious arguments, arguers tend to attack the opponents instead of the opponents' evidence or reasoning.

For example, "Andreas Fisher has written several articles trying to argue that online pornography has a negative effect on women. But Andreas Fisher is ugly and bad, so why should we listen to her argument?" The arguers are trying to attack her beauty as being ugly to say no to her argument, instead of trying to prove that her argument is wrong by having good reasoning and evidence to support it. Her beauty has nothing to do with the strength of her argument. Thus, using her beauty as the evidence is fallacious.

In tuquoque, the arguers are trying to show why we should believe this claim if the person who makes the claim also does what they are arguing and so the opponent's argument should not be taken into account.

For instance, there is a family where a father smokes and is always trying to tell his son that smoking is bad. He has given a lot of good reasons why his son should not smoke such as it damages health, costs and so forth. However, the son replies back to his father that "I won't accept what you have just said because you also used to smoke when you were my age." You did it too. The thing here is the father has done something that he is arguing about, so it has no bearing on the premises he is putting in his argument. Therefore, the son's response to his father's argument is fallacious.

The important thing we can do to avoid this type of fallacy is that we should focus on the opponent's reasoning or evidence rather than their personal character. However, if we are about to make an argument about a person's character, it is no longer fallacious to focus on his/her character.

Ad Populum

The meaning of this Latin word is "to the people." There are many versions of ad populum but it is usually a type of fallacy in which the arguer takes advantage of the desire that most people have to be liked and uses that desire to get the audience to accept the argument. In other words, the arguer tries to persuade other people to believe in his/her argument because everyone else does.

For example, same-sex marriage is simply immoral. 70% of Americans think so. The opinion of most Americans may influence the American government in determining what law they should have, but it is not certainly relevant to the opponent's argument in determining whether same-sex marriage is moral or immoral. The arguer is trying to make us agree with his/her conclusion by appealing to our desire to fit with the American people.

We have to ensure that we do not try to make other people believe in our conclusion just because many others agree. Always remember that something well-known is always the right one to follow.

Straw Man

A man who is made of straw is easier to knock over than a real man. An effective way to strengthen our argument is by anticipating what argument our opponent might make. For the straw man fallacy, the arguers try to make the weak version of the argument that the opponent might make. The arguers sometimes exaggerate or misrepresent an opponent's position. The idea of this argument is to make the opponent's argument look weak so that people will accept our argument. Therefore, the true position of the opponent's argument is not real anymore because it has been exaggerated and misrepresented. It becomes weak and easily rejected and criticized.

For example, there is a conversation between a student and teacher. The student tells the teacher that he thinks some of Donald Trump's position has virtue. The teacher says that he cannot believe that his student supports racist ideas. So here, the teacher assumes that his student will not say something good about Donald Trump because he thinks everyone is against the idea of racism.

The straw man fallacy is so common that it ranks top on our list of the top ten fallacies of all time (see inside front cover). One person will say he wants to eliminate the words "under God" from the Pledge of Allegiance and his opponent will act as if he wants to eliminate the entire pledge. A conservative will oppose tightening emission standards for sulfur dioxide and a liberal will accuse him of wanting to relax the standards. A Democratic congresswoman will say she opposes cutting taxes and her Republican opponent will accuse her of wanting to raise taxes.

False Dichotomy

In this type of fallacy, the arguer will try to set up a situation that looks like there are only two possible options that we have to choose from. Then, they will eliminate one of them and make the one left the best choice that you can possibly make. Therefore, we choose the one left or agree with the conclusion. In fact, there are not just two choices, and if we had to think about them, we probably would choose the one left that the arguer recommended.

For example, "you will need to go to a party in the club with me or you will get bored staying at home." This is an example of a false dichotomy. The arguer tries to convince the audience to go to the party as no one wants to stay at home and get bored. The suggestion here is that there are two choices. One is to go to the party and the second one is to stay at home and get bored. The argument neglects to mention the possibility that we might go to do something else besides going to the party or find something else fun to do at home. There are actually, many more possibilities that we can choose to indulge in.

In order to make a good decision and avoid false dichotomy, you need to observe closely the arguments and try to see if there are really only two alternatives available for you to choose. You can ask yourself if there are other options or possibilities besides the two.

The Genetic Fallacy

The genetic fallacy occurs when we tend to reject the claim (or urge others to do so) on the basis of its origin, history, and sources rather than its recent meaning or context. They tend to overlook the current position of the claim in the current context and usually, refer to the earlier context as the basis to refute the claim. The claim is accepted as true or false based on the origin of the claim. In genetic fallacy, the source of the claim can be other kinds of entities such as a club, a political party, or an industrial group. For instance, the doctor is overweight, so I don't believe anything he says about improving health. Here, I tend to reject what the doctor said in regards to improving health because he is simply overweight. I think if he cannot even have good health, how can he possibly make me healthy?

Rhetoric

When you tell a kid that you went waterboarding at Guantanamo Bay, they may think that you had one of the best holidays ever. Little do they know that Guantanamo Bay is a prison and waterboarding is a form of torture made to simulate drowning. Similar language is used all over the world. "Self-injurious behavior incidents" means attempted suicide. "Detainee" means prisoner. When you hear that a company is "downsizing," you know that someone is getting fired. "Ethnic cleansing" is little more than deportation or genocide.

What we have to say may be important, but the words we choose to use can be just as important. The examples we gave are cases of a certain type of linguistic coercion, an attempt to make you adopt a certain attitude towards a topic. You may be surprised how you can phrase the same exact ideas differently and people will react differently. The words we use have tremendous persuasive power, or what we have called their rhetorical force or emotive meaning. The words we say have the power to express and elicit images, feelings, and emotional associations.

Rhetoric refers to the study of persuasive writing. In this context, it means the use of linguistic techniques to influence beliefs, attitudes, and behaviors. Here is another example:

"Does Julia still owe over $5,000 on her credit card?" and "Does Julia owe a little over $5,000 on her credit card?"

Just by reading this alone, you can tell that there is a major difference between the two questions: the severity. In fact, there is no difference between the two questions, but you feel that the former is a lot more serious. If we allow ourselves to be affected by rhetoric, we fall short as critical thinkers.

Of course, there is nothing wrong with trying to prove a point using rhetoric, using well-chosen, rhetorically effective words and phrases. Good writers do this all the time. However, as a critical thinker, you need to be able to distinguish in an argument its logical force and psychological force through rhetoric. Applying rhetoric to your writing is not wrong. The point here is not to omit arguments or reasoning that is presented in rhetorically charged language, and we are not suggesting you remove all sorts of rhetoric from your own language.

In this section, we will identify common rhetoric to help you identify them as they are presented in an argument, so you can analyze information presented to you objectively.

Euphemisms and Dysphemisms

Language allows us to say the same thing several times over, and all of them make the listener feel differently. It is the difference between a poet and a politician. Until recently, the term "used car" means a car that is not new. Now, these cars are called "pre-owned," which does not make much sense. The dealers hope that by using different terms, the buyers would feel more inclined to buy their cars because "used" is such a strong word. The term "pre-owned" is a euphemism.

Euphemism is a neutral or positive expression used to hide negative associations. Mainly used by politicians, mass media, and advertisement, euphemisms are key in affecting our attitudes. People may feel less strongly about the assassination of a foreign leader if the act is referred to as "neutralization." People fighting against the government can be labeled as "freedom fighters." A "tax hike" sounds a lot worse than "revenue enhancement program." The United States Department of Defense used to be called the "Department of War."

On the other spectrum, we have dysphemism. Dysphemisms are used to elicit a negative response or attitude from readers or listeners toward something. It can also be used to downplay the positive association it has. So, "freedom fighters" become "terrorists."

Both euphemisms and dysphemisms are often used in deceptive ways. While deceptive, they can be helpful when used properly such as backing a good cause. They allow us to approach a sensitive subject indirectly by preventing a hostile reaction, therefore, grinding a discussion to a halt. They can also be used just to be more polite. For example, "dead" is rough compared to "passed on" So, its uses can also be legitimate.

Rhetorical Definitions and Rhetorical Explanations

Definitions are intended to clarify meaning and enhance our understanding. When they are loaded with rhetoric, they are intended to change our attitude toward something. When it comes to abortion, how do you define it? Some say it is giving women the chance to live without the burden of raising children, which makes abortion a good thing. Others may define abortion as the murder of an unborn child. So, rhetorical definitions are intended to sway our attitude toward something based on the definition.

Rhetorical explanations are also similar to rhetorical definitions. This time, they are under the guise of explanations. Suppose that your friend lost a fight. He would feel less humiliated if you say that he lost because he was too cautious instead of saying that he lost his nerve. Both are the same because the fact is that he lost the fight, but how it happened can be described differently.

Stereotypes

A Stereotype is a thought or image of a group of people based on little to no evidence. Thinking that men are insensitive (or stoic if you want to put it that way), women are emotional (or expressive), that gay men are effeminate, and lesbians are man-haters are all stereotypes. When you group people under a name or description, especially ones that begin with "the" such as the Communists, the Liberals, the right-wing, the Jews, etc, such labeling often result in stereotyping.

Language that reduces people or things to categories can entice the audience to accept a claim towards those categories without much thought. It can also be used to make quick judgments concerning groups of individuals about whom they know so little.

Stereotypes are mainly used in the political spectrum, which can also involve the ad hominem fallacy. For instance, if you call someone a "left-wing extremist" to defame someone in a political debate, you are using a negative stereotype and an ad hominem (personal attack). So, if we attach a positive stereotype to someone, you create a good impression of that person. If you say that someone is a gentleman, you attach a favorable stereotype, that of a gentleman, to that person.

From where do we get all of our stereotypes? Everywhere, but mainly from the media such as literature, movies, or the news. They are often supported by a variety of prejudices and group interests. Initially, the Native American tribes of the Great Plains were considered to be noble by many white people up until the mid-nineteenth century. From there, white people were more interested in getting these Native Americans to leave, which created a conflict between the two groups. It escalated further and further, and popular literature back then started to describe the Native Americans as subhuman creatures – savages, to put them in a bad light. This stereotype supported the interest of white people. Conflicts generally give birth to some derogatory stereotypes for both sides. Psychologically, it is easier to kill without the pangs of conscience if that person is considered to be less of a human than us. Stereotyping is a lot easier if there are racial differences as well.

When blood pressure gets up and tension is so high, the fact that nothing could have been further from the truth never dawned on anyone. In the heat of the moment is when you need to restrain yourself and think critically of everything. When both sides are armed, and people lose their minds, heads will start rolling unless someone can deescalate the situation.

Innuendo

When we communicate with other people, we normally have certain expectations and assumptions. For instance, if your teacher says that everybody passed the exam, you would automatically assume that she meant the whole class or those who took the exam. She did not mean that everyone in the world passed the exam. These expectations and assumptions basically give us the context of the situation as it pans out, allowing us to follow along without the other person having to explain everything in meticulous detail. Realistically, no one could be bothered to explain everything all the time, especially in casual conversation. These expectations are important to the success of communication. Innuendo plays on these expectations to sway the opinions of listeners and readers.

For example: "Ladies and gentlemen, I am proof that there is at least one candidate in this race who does not have a drug problem."

Now, this statement is not saying explicitly that any of the opponents of the speaker has drug problems. In fact, the speaker is not denying the fact that other opponents might not have such a problem since the speaker said "at least one candidate." Still, the problem here is that there is no need to say this unless someone among the group has a drug problem. So, the speaker just casts suspicion on all of his opponents. This kind of innuendo aims to get a point across without saying it out loud.

As you can see, the use of innuendo allows us to suggest something bad about something or someone without actually saying it. For example, if someone asks you whether Jane is telling the truth, you may reply, "Yes, this time." This suggests that maybe Jane is not as truthful as the asker may be led to believe. You can say that "Ron is usually helpful," which may suggest that he is sometimes incompetent and unhelpful.

Innuendo does not always have to sound like a neutral statement. You can say something positive about someone and still condemn them at the same time. For example, you can just praise someone a bit when you should have praised them a lot more. In doing so, we hint that the person does not deserve high praise at all, devaluing their efforts. This is another kind of innuendo. For example, after reading a letter of recommendation saying, "Mr. Watson has done some good work for us, I guess," you are not convinced, are you? This letter does not inspire you to hire Mr. Watson immediately. Alternatively, saying "He's been useful so far," or "Surprisingly, he seems very astute," might put him in a worse spot because you assume that he might have done something bad as well to warrant such bland praise. You may notice that the information in these statements is not negative at all. The innuendo lies between the lines, so you need to develop a keen eye to spot it.

Loaded Questions

Another form of innuendo is the loaded question. If you overheard someone ask, "Have you always loved to gamble?" you would naturally assume that the person being questioned did, in fact, love to gamble. This assumption is independent of whether the person answered yes or no, for it underlies the question itself. Every question rests on assumptions. Even an innocent question like "What time is it?" depends on the assumption that the listener speaks English and has some means of finding out the time, for instance. A loaded question is less innocent, however. It rests on one or more unwarranted or unjustified assumptions. The world's oldest example, "Have you stopped beating your wife?" rests on the assumption that the person asked has in the past beaten his wife. If there is no reason to think that this assumption is true, then the question is loaded.

Another form of innuendo is the loaded question. If someone were to ask you, "Have you always loved to drink?" you would assume that the other person thinks that you love to drink. This assumption is there regardless of the answer because it underlies the question itself. That is not to say that only loaded questions have assumptions. Innocent questions such as "What day is it today?" assume that the one being questioned speaks English and knows how to find out the day. Every question rests on some sort of assumptions. However, a loaded question has a less innocent assumption. It is based on one or more unjustified or unwarranted. The best example we have here is, "Have you stopped beating your wife?" Now, this question rests on the assumption that the person being questioned has beaten his wife in the past.

How do you identify a loaded question? If there is no reason to think that the assumption is true, then the question is most likely a loaded question. How do you answer a loaded question? Jordan Peterson's interview with Cathy Newman is the perfect example here. When she asked him loaded questions, Jordan took a step back and rephrased the questions, taking away their unwarranted assumption. So, someone asks you whether you have stopped beating your wife, just take a step back and say that you have never beaten your wife.

Weaslers

Weaslers, as the name suggests, protect the person making a claim from criticism by somewhat watering it down, weakening the claim itself, to allow the person to "weasel" his way out if the claim is challenged. They are the linguistic methods of hedging a bet, in a way. Weaslers are commonly used in an advertisement, as you may already be very familiar with. For example, an ad may claim that "Four out of five dentists surveyed recommend sugarless gum for their patients who chew gum." Here, the claim has two weasling expressions.

The first offender is the word "surveyed." The advertisement does not tell us the criteria for choosing the dentists surveyed. Were they chosen randomly or were they dentists who may not be unfavorably disposed toward gum chewing? To make matters worse, there is nothing indicating that the sample of dentists represents the general population of dentists. As far as we know, the sample size could be five, and four of them recommend sugarless gum. Because of this, even if every other dentist on the planet called this ad out, saying that it does not represent the entire population, the author could just say that they only spoke about the surveyed dentists, not all dentists. So, the author could get away with making this claim.

The second offender is "for their patients who chew gum." Did you notice that the ad does not say that any dentists believe that you should not chew gum altogether? The ad only suggests two alternatives: sugar or sugarless gum. Suppose you were to ask the dentists this, "If a patient of yours is adamant about chewing gum, would you prefer that he or she chews gum with sugar in it or sugarless gum?" When you phrase the question this way, of course, any dentists would say that sugarless gum would be a better option. If you were to ask whether people should chew gum without sugar in it, they will say that you might as well not chew gum at all. In this case, the weaslers allow the advertisement author to get away from what is an unqualified recommendation for sugarless gum using facts that have nothing to do to support the recommendation.

Okay, let us make something up. Let's say, a statistic like 99 percent of European doctors don't believe that vaccination is a contributing cause of autism in children, and the remaining 1 percent are convinced. We can then say that "some doctors are convinced that vaccination causes autism in children," and get away with it because we cannot be held accountable for having said something false. Even if our claim is misleading to someone who does know have an in-depth knowledge of the subject, the word "some" allowed us to weasel our way out.

Other words such as "possible," "maybe," and "perhaps," have many uses in the rhetorical context. For one, they can be used to create innuendo to plant a suggestion without explicitly saying it out loud. Doing so allows us to create a claim that is hard to defend. For example, we can say that Tom is a liar without saying it exactly. We can just say that "Tom may be a liar." We can also say that "It is possible that Tom is a liar," which is true for all of us anyway. We lie at some point in our lives. We can also say "Perhaps Tom is a liar," without a problem. These are some examples of how weaslers can be used to create innuendo.

Of course, just because those words are used does not mean that the author is trying to slip in an innuendo to create a way for him to weasel out of. These words can also be used to bring some important qualifications to bear on a claim. It all depends on the context in which the weasel is used. For instance, a detective who is evaluating all the possible angles on a homicide case and just heard Tom's account of the event might say to the police, "Of course, it is possible that Tom is lying." This is not the case of weasling. The detective here is simply exercising due care. So, other words that can be used as weaslers can also be used legitimately. Other qualifying phrases such as "it may well be that" "it is arguable that" and so on can also be used as weaslers. Of course, qualifying phrases are not created equal, and some suggest weasling more than others. For instance, "some would say that" is more commonly used as a weaseling device, although it can be used for an honest purpose in the right context.

So, how can you spot weasling? Well, the only thing you can do is to be careful when qualifying phrases are used. Think whether the speaker or writer is posing a reasonable qualification, using a bit of innuendo, or trying to create a way he could weasel out of? You can only assess what the speaker or writer has said, the context, and the subject itself to determine if the use of a qualifying phrase has an honest intention.

Down players

Downplaying is an attempt to make something or someone look unimportant or insignificant. Downplaying can include stereotypes, rhetorical comparisons, rhetorical explanations, and innuendo. For instance, if you say "Don't mind what Ms. Hank says in class; she's a liberal," you have just downplayed Ms. Hank. This attaches a stereotype to whatever Ms. Hank has to say. You can also downplay someone or something through careful phrasing using certain words or other devices. Using our previous example, you can say, "Don't mind what Ms. Hank says in class; she's just another liberal." The phrase "just another" denigrates Ms. Hank further. So, down players are words or other devices used in order to make someone or something seemingly insignificant.

Other than "just" and "another," two other common down players is "mere" and "merely." If your friend Fred tells you that he has a yellow belt in the Tibetan martial art and that his brother has a "mere" green belt, you would normally assume that a yellow belt is ranked higher than a green belt. What we don't know is that a yellow belt is probably ranked lower than a green belt, and he was probably implying that his brother only made little progress although he has been practicing for several years. Here, we can say that Fred's use of the word "mere" gives you the right to make that assumption. Whether or not it is in Fred's intention to not mention that his brother had more experience and is actually ranked higher, Fred was trying to downplay his brother's accomplishment.

The term "so-called" is another standard downplayer. We might say, for example, that the woman who made the diagnosis is a "so-called doctor," which downplays her credentials as a physician. Quotation marks can be used to accomplish the same thing:

You can say that the man who performed the surgery is a "so-called surgeon," which diminishes his credibility as a physician. In written communication, the placement of the quotation marks is also critical because they can be used to emphasize something or downplay something. Take a look at this example:

He got his "degree" from a law school.

The use of quotation marks to downplay something is not to be confused with their other use: to indicate irony. This is an example of irony:

Jack "borrowed" Ben's pen, and Ben hasn't seen it since.

In our second example here, the idea is not to downplay the act of Jack borrowing Ben's pen. The quotation marks are used here to indicate that it was actually not a case of borrowing. The marks around the words "so-called" and "degree" in our previous example are intended to be downplayers, reducing the significance and importance of their subjects. Downplayers are quite obvious, so you should not have too much trouble spotting them.

Other conjunctions such as "still," "but," "however," and "nevertheless" can also be used to downplay claims. These conjunctions are a lot harder to spot because they blend in so well with the claim. Take a look at these examples and try to spot the difference:

Ex 1: Of course, the chemical leak at the plant was a horrible tragedy; however, we should not forget that these pesticide plants are the key in our Green Revolution initiative dedicated to feeding millions of people across the globe.

Ex 2: While it is true that the pesticide plants hold the key to the success of our Green Revolution initiative which has fed millions of people worldwide, it was just such a plant that developed a leak and caused such a horrible tragedy.

The differences between them are not as obvious as those in the cases of "so-called" and "mere," but you can already tell where the sympathies of the authors' are.

Another way to notice the use of downplayers is to observe the context in which the claim is used. Think of the remark, "Mark won only by five votes." The word "only" here may or may not downplay Mark's victory, depending on how thin the five-vote margin is. Let's say that a million people voted and Mark won by five, then the use of "only" is perfectly appropriate. It is not a downplay because Mark literally just won by the skin of his teeth. Alternatively, if the vote was in a committee of nineteen, then five is a substantial margin. Here, Mark would have twelve votes to seven, if everyone votes. The ratio is almost two to one. So, using the word "only" here is obviously a sly device used to make Mark's victory less important than it deserves.

Before you get in trouble, we are not saying that slanters cannot and should not be used altogether. You can use them to give a flair to your writing. What you should avoid is being unconsciously manipulated by these slanters. Finding a well-placed down player is a real gem, and you can appreciate how much thought the writer has put into trying to conceal this. Be aware of how these downplayers, subtle or not, can have an effect on you. In doing so, you can protect yourself from being manipulated by a clever speaker or writer.

Sarcasm

We are all familiar with sarcasm. This kind of rhetorical device is used to ridicule others. It is a powerful rhetorical tool because many of us hate being laughed at as it makes us look incompetent. So, do not be discouraged if someone laughs at your own expense. Just because they laugh does not mean that your argument is any less valid. They haven't even raised their objections to your position.

One might just laugh outright at a claim ("Send aid to Russia? Hah! Good one!"), laugh at another claim because it reminds us of the first ("Take away the Second Amendment Right? Sure, when hell freezes over! Har, har, har!"), tell an unrelated joke to distract you from the discussion, use sarcastic language, or just laugh at the person who is trying to get their point across.

When you are in a debate or watching one, remember that the person who can make the audience laugh the most with the funniest lines has a higher chance of winning the debate. Critical thinkers see differently because they see the difference between arguments and entertainment. That is not to say that there is anything wrong with entertainment in a debate, of course. Being serious all the time makes it boring anyway, even if both sides have good arguments.

Hyperbole

On the opposite spectrum of down players, we have hyperbole. As its name suggests, it is an extravagant overstatement. A claim that exaggerates for effect is considered to be hyperbole, depending on the language used and the points it is trying to get across.

For example, it is a hyperbole if someone were to describe a hangnail as a serious injury. It is a hyperbole if someone used the word "fascists" to describe parents who insist that their children have to be home by midnight. Of course, not all colorful or strong language is hyperbole. It depends on the context in which the claim is made. For instance, you can say that "Oscar Peterson is an astoundingly inventive pianist." It is a strong claim, but it is not a hyperbole. It is not that extravagant. But if you were to say "Oscar Peterson is the most inventive musician mankind has ever seen," that is hyperbole. It is beyond emphasis because how can you know that Oscar Peterson is more inventive than Mozart?

Hyperbole can be used in dysphemisms and rhetorical comparisons. When we use the dysphemisms "extremist" or "greedy" to describe the views of a member from an opposing political party, we are using hyperbole. If we say that the general is less informed than an orange that is hyperbole used in a rhetorical comparison. Similarly, you can use hyperbole in rhetorical explanations and definitions.

Hyperbole is sometimes used in ridicule or sarcasm. If it uses any form of exaggeration, the ridicule is a hyperbole. In our previous example, saying that the general is less informed than an orange is hyperbole used in a rhetorical comparison to ridicule that official.

A claim can be hyperbolic even though the author does not use excessively emotive words or phrases. In our previous examples, neither of them use such language. The word "astoundingly" is the most emotive word in our claim about Peterson, but it is not a hyperbole. Still, a claim can be a hyperbole if we use such language. Saying that "parents who are strict about hanging out with friends are fascists" is a hyperbole, but if we were to replace the word "fascists" with "mean," the claim is still strong and a bit exaggerated, but not hyperbolic. So, when the language becomes excessive and colorful, then the claim is probably hyperbole. It depends on your judgment of the context in which the claim is made.

You can already tell that hyperbole is not subtle in its appearance, but its effect is a lot more subtle. It may even sway your opinions unconsciously. Try as you might to reject it, which is easy to do because it is so blatant, but you may be moved in the direction of the basic claim. For instance, you can reject the claim saying that Oscar Peterson is the most inventive musician, but you may now think that he is a very talented musician anyway. If not, why would someone make such an exaggerated claim about him? Suppose someone says that Taylor Swift is the best singer of all time, and you reject that claim, you at least think that Taylor Swift is a talented singer. This is where you need to be cautious because any claim is just as worthless without reason to support it. Just because the claim is wild does not mean that you should accept it more than ordinary, unsupported claims.

Proof Surrogates

A proof surrogate is an expression used to suggest that there is evidence or authority for a claim without really citing or presenting them. In some cases, we cannot prove the claim we are trying to assert, but we can at least hint that there is proof or evidence available without actually committing ourselves to them. Phrases such as "many studies" or "informed sources say" are some of the most common ways to make a claim suddenly more authoritative. The thing is, no sources are cited. Who are the sources? How do we know if they are legitimate? How does the person making the claim know that they are informed? "It's obvious that" is also regularly used and it sometimes precedes a claim that is not obvious at all. But when we are told that something is obvious, we may hold back our objections because we think that it is obvious to everyone else but you and because we do not want to appear denser than the next guy. The audience may also have the same thought. In advertisements, "studies show" is often used. Again, this alone does not tell us anything about how many studies were conducted, how good they are, who did them, as well as any other important information.

Remember, proof surrogates are only surrogates. They are not meant to be considered as real proof or evidence. The proof or evidence might exist, but the claim is still unsupported until they are presented. At best, proof surrogates suggest sloppy research. At worst, they suggest propaganda.

Rhetorical Analogies and Misleading Comparisons

Misleading comparisons are also commonly used, mainly by politicians to promote their agenda. For example, Robert Kittle, who was an editorial page editor for the San Diego Union-Tribune, said that the Social Security system is a Ponzi scheme. If you do not know, a Ponzi scheme is a pyramid scheme intended to get as much money out of its members as possible. What Robert did there was known as a rhetorical analogy. The rhetorical analogy is defined as the comparison of two things to make one of them seem better or worse than it is. Of course, analogies are often used to help you explain something, not necessarily to manipulate.

For instance, if you are trying to explain rugby to a friend of yours who knows nothing about it, you may compare it to football. In our example here, Kittle's comparison is not intended to explain to the reader, but rather to persuade and sway their opinions. Ponzi scheme is such a strong and negative term, and calling something a Ponzi scheme puts it in a bad spot.

People often replace arguments with rhetorical analogies. It is not hard to see why, really. You need facts to prove something is true. In our example, you need to do extensive research to prove that Social Security is financially unsustainable. If anything, it is more convenient to just call it a Ponzi scheme altogether because it may be just as effective anyway. This kind of persuasion works really well as you can persuade the listener without the need to show actual proof. You can also make rhetorical analogies using metaphors and similes, and they still make the audience feel a certain way.

Comparisons also fall under rhetorical analogies. For example, you can say that you have a higher chance of dying in a car crash than in a plane crash. This is a creative way of getting your point across, but just because that is true does not mean that it is a reason for accepting that point.

If we are not careful, we can fall victim to some comparisons. A great example is the vagueness present in advertisements. Their slogans say something like "New and improved formula," or "Now 50 percent larger," or "Quietest by far." With a little scrutiny, you can already tell that these claims are worth little. We have talked about vagueness before. How is it new and improved? 50 percent larger compared to what? Quietest by what standard? Unless the changes are spelled out explicitly, telling you exactly what has been improved, these claims are worth very little.

While we are on the topic of comparison, you may be familiar with discounts at the mall and other sales events. "50% off!" the banners read, "Buy one get one!" Oftentimes, people will flock to buy whatever is on sale, even though they may not have much use for whatever they are buying. But why do people buy things they do not have a use for? You see, we learn how to exploit opportunities or scarcity. We believe that the discount is going to be a once in a lifetime opportunity, so we take it. Being opportunistic is good, but the problem is that we do not think much of the result. Companies learn to exploit this weakness and put up discounts all the time. Their profit margin per product may go down, but the sales will go so high that it compensates for the loss. That is, of course, if they did not mark up the price before the "discount" event. If you sell lollipops for $0.25 a pop, people may not buy them. If you put up a discount sign saying that you are selling four lollipops for $1, you may sell more than you think. What do we learn here? Similar to the example we gave above, it is worth to stop and think carefully about the opportunities you are presented with. Sure, that pair of shoes is 50% cheaper, but it's not worth buying it if you won't use them any time soon anyway.

When faced with comparisons, it is worth asking yourself these five questions. They include references to omissions and distortions, which are some of the most subtle forms of rhetorical devices.

1. Is important information missing? Of course, learning that the unemployment rate went down to virtually zero is a good thing, but the result may be because most of the workforce has just given up on looking for a job. If somcone tells you that 75 percent of heroin addicts once smoked marijuana, that does not mean much either without more information. Over 75 percent of

heroin addicts have listened to the Beatles at least once, too. That does not tell us anything. A U.S. Congressional Representative, Wally Herger, told his constituents that Social Security is in dire straits, saying once that there were 42 workers to support a single retiree, the number has now gone down to 3. From the get-go, what he claimed seemed ominous. What Representative Herger failed to mention is that the 42-to-1 ratio was only present at the start of Social Security, before many people retired. He also failed to mention that the 3-to-1 ratio has been constant for the last two decades or so, during which Social Security has accumulated a surplus.

2. Is the same standard of comparison used? Are the same practices of reporting and recording used? The fluctuation of the unemployment rate

does not tell much if the government changes the way it calculates unemployment, which actually happens sometimes. It is like saying that an athlete managed to jump as far as 200 meters when a meter to you is one centimeter to another. Comparisons cannot be used unless they are measured by the same standard. Back in 1993, the number of people in the U.S. who were HIV positive suddenly skyrocketed. Was there an outbreak? Had a new form of the AIDS virus appeared? No, and no. The federal government just expanded the definition of AIDS to include many other indicator conditions. Suddenly, 50,000 more people were considered to be HIV positive overnight.

3. Are the items comparable? It is obviously difficult to compare who is the better bodybuilder if one of them used

steroids and the other did not, or if one had a coach or better equipment. It is hard to draw a conclusion from the fact that this May's retail business activity is much lower compared to last May's if a tornado suddenly hit the local area, causing heavy rain and flooding for the whole month. It is hard to draw a conclusion from the fact that there are more male deaths in traffic accidents compared to female when men often drive farther and longer hours than women. Comparing share values of two mutual funds in the last decade will not tell you any new information if the comparison itself does not consider the difference in fees. So, the comparison should only be done when the two things share values.

4. Is the comparison expressed as an average? The average rainfall in Seattle is about the same as that in Kansas City.

But you'll spend more time in the rain in Seattle because it rains there twice as often as it does in Kansas City.

5. Is the comparison expressed as an average? If a company reports that the average salaries of most of its employees have doubled over the last decade, you may assume that it is a great place to work. That is not always the case though. The increase may be caused by the conversion of half-time to full-time staff and firing the rest. Be wary of comparisons that involve averages because they often omit important details, just because they involve averages. The average rainfall in Seattle is roughly the same as that of Kansas City, but you will spend more time in the rain living in Seattle because it rains twice as often, compared to Kansas City. Averages are just measures of central tendency, and there are different kinds

of measures or averages. For example, take the average cost of a new house in your area. Let us assume that it is $100,000. If that is the mean, then it is the total of the sales prices divided by the number of houses sold, which may be different from the median. The median is an average that is the halfway figure (half the houses cost more and half cost less). The mode is the most common sales price, which can be again, different. If you are offered an average of anything, be very cautious.

Persuasion Using Visual Images

In this age, where people can edit a picture of Justin Bieber into a potato, it is much easier to take photographic evidence at face value. Back then, you could not just edit digital photos. Still, there were all kinds of things that could be done to manipulate an image. Even without the tools to edit photos, people still managed to change a viewer's perception of what was going on in the photo. In some cases, you do not even need to edit the photos and videos to create a mistaken impression in the viewer.

Back in 2005, Terri Schiavo, a Florida woman, became the center of a controversy regarding whether she was in a Persistent Vegetative State (PVS) and could be expected to regain consciousness, let alone recover. Her family members took a video of her, which showed that she appeared to be responding to the presence of her mother. A heart surgeon and majority leader of the U.S. Senate, Bill First, also saw the videotape and claimed that Ms. Schiavo seemed to be responding to visual stimuli. On the other hand, other doctors including her own also said that these facial expressions were often displayed by those in PVS, and were not necessarily a conscious response. After her death, an autopsy was conducted showing that Ms. Schiavo's brain had shrunk to half its original size. What was left was a severely damaged brain. Other than that, her visual cortex was damaged as well, which meant that she had been blind for quite some time before her eventual death. The possibility of having anything like consciousness near the end of her life was a medical impossibility.

This is how a simple videotape can be ambiguous. It is open to more than one interpretation, even if it was a raw, unedited video clip. Many viewers can have a mistaken impression which leads them to make false claims. Of course, photos, videos, and other imagery cannot be true or false per se, but claims based on them can be.

Some people perform image manipulations of various sorts to try to create mistaken impressions. How can you identify them? These images can be the result of:

- Deliberately manipulating an image (e.g., adding, deleting, combining)
- Using unaltered images but with misleading captions
- Deliberately selected camera angles that distort information
- Lack of authority (i.e., author name, credentials); inconsistency when compared to official images
- Imagery taken from movies: out of context, they are given false descriptions
- Imagery taken of models purported to be the real thing
- Imagery that is genuine and unadulterated but "staged"
- 100% digital fabrications

It is unrealistic to expect people to be able to identify edited photos and videos wherever they appear, especially with the current technology. No one can do it, to be honest. Some images are so carefully edited that no one but the creator himself knows that they are fake.

So, what can a critical thinker do here? You do what every other critical thinker does: be careful. While there are plenty of people out there trying to inform and educate you, know that there are many more whose objective is to fool you. Take everything with a grain of salt and do not take everything at face value.

Chapter 8: How Critical Thinking Affects Your Life

Critical thinking is a general thinking skill. In whatever we want and choose to do, the ability to think clearly and rationally is important. Critical thinking is obviously necessary when you have a career in finance, research, education, management, or in the legal field. Still, that does not mean critical thinking skills are restricted to any subject area. Being able to think clearly and solve problems systematically is an important asset to have, no matter which career you are pursuing.

Critical thinking is very important in the new knowledge economy. Information technology is also important in the global knowledge economy nowadays as it is driven by these two factors. Plus, we need to be prepared to deal with constant and rapid changes promptly and effectively. As the fluctuation of the worldwide economy increases, so does the demand for flexible intellectual skills such as the ability to analyze information and utilize diverse sources of knowledge to solve problems. Critical thinking skills help promote these intellectual skills and are essential in the ever-changing workplace.

Critical thinking helps improve language and presentation skills. The ability to think clearly and systematically can help improve the way we present our ideas. Critical thinking also improves our comprehension abilities in learning how to analyze the logical structure of texts.

Creativity also comes from critical thinking. One may need to use ideas and information differently in order to generate creative solutions. Critical thinking can also be utilized to evaluate new ideas, determine whether or not they are useful and relevant, and select the best one or change them if needed.

Good critical thinking is the foundation of democracy and science. Objective use of information and reasoning in experiments is fundamental. In order to run a liberal democracy properly, all citizens need to be able to think critically about social issues that lead to proper governance and to overcome biases and prejudice in society.

We do not want people to just focus on learning and do their work well only in the classroom as the fundamental objective of education is to create a desire to learn more beyond the academic school year. Critical thinking is a lifelong learning process and critical thinkers are also lifelong learners.

We need to start from the basics if we want to discover how critical thinking is related to lifelong learning. Lifelong learning is a self-motivated desire in learning that persists throughout our entire lifetime. However, what makes these people want to continue learning for their entire lifetime? It must be not just about desiring to become a success and for survival. To keep learning, we need to maintain our interest in learning by making sure that the process of learning itself is relevant, focused, and practical. For instance, which of the following have you done recently or in the past?

- Read a book and learned something new
- Watched a YouTube tutorial video on how to fix something
- Participated in any kind of class, course, or training
- Searched on how to do school assignments online
- Learned something from other people including a tutor or a mentor

All of these actions have something in common. These are the activities that a critical thinker might take to fix a problem or answer the question. To people who think critically, all of the information and knowledge from every side is essential and needed. Both critical thinking and lifelong learning share inherent qualities that are the ability to see potential in any approach to learning. Learning for a lifetime shows itself in a number of different ways. The above examples are some of them. We can also learn from other people through socializing, gaining experience in any activities, or simply making observations or mistakes. So, we can develop critical thinking by practicing it whenever we can.

Chapter 9: Conclusion

That's about it. With all of the knowledge acquired in this book, you are well on your way to improving your critical thinking skills and identifying fallacy and rhetoric in other peoples' arguments.

The key here is to think systematically and go slow if you must. It is always better to think slowly than to decide incorrectly. Having good critical thinking skills puts you way above others in professional and personal fields as you can decide and act in a way that best benefits everyone. One cannot stress enough how important it is to develop your critical thinking skills, especially in this day and age where manipulation and misinformation run rampant.

Thankfully, you are no longer a victim of this falsehood. Your life will be significantly improved thanks to your new way of thinking. Give yourself a pat on the back for reading this far, and good luck on your journey.

www.ingramcontent.com/pod-product-compliance
Lightning Source LLC
Chambersburg PA
CBHW071236070526
44583CB00017B/2203